SENIOR MOMENTS

HALL OF FAME

REMEMBERING THE TITANS OF FORGETFULNESS

TOM FRIEDMAN

Author of *1,000 Unforgettable Senior Moments*

ISBN-10: 1480139823
EAN-13: 9781480139824

"May the Titans of Forgetfulness lose your address."

—*Traditional blessing of some misplaced ancient civilization*

THE TITANS OF FORGETFULNESS

PLEASE WAIT HERE
FOR YOUR TOUR GUIDE

Ah, there you are at last. Welcome to the Senior Moments Hall of Fame, dedicated to the Titans of Forgetfulness. Here, in this hallowed place, we pay tribute to those profoundly absentminded people who inspired countless senior moment sufferers just like you.

In a very special way, our Hall is your Hall, or vice versa, or whatever.

But please, before we begin our tour, take a few moments to look around and ooh-and-ah. As you can see, the Senior Moments Hall of Fame is modeled after an ancient Greek temple to reinforce the gravitas of our mission. (It also enables us to offer visitors a once-in-a-lifetime opportunity to buy a handsome bronze replica in our gift shop, or better yet, two, since you're bound to lose the first one.)

And now it's finally time to enter the world-famous...

ANTEROOM OF INTRODUCTION

Who *are* the Titans of Forgetfulness, and how were they selected? Both are excellent questions, which I'm sure you would have asked eventually after you thought of them.

Simply put, the Titans of Forgetfulness are people of historic stature who had senior moments that were even worse than yours. And yet these spectacular memory lapses did not prevent our Titans from blazing new paths in science, creating great art, amassing or frittering away enormous wealth, wielding tremendous power, winning glittering prizes, setting new records in sports, or spreading their wisdom far and wide — even if they had trouble figuring out exactly where they were, or how they got there.

It is thanks to these heroes and heroines of forgetfulness that each of you will now be able to say honestly and proudly after your next embarrassing lapse of memory or bout of absentmindedness, "I may be forgetful, but I'm nothing compared to Sir Isaac Newton!"

Let us begin with some basics, shall we?

On your left is an animatronics display of forgetful folks of all ages. Notice how life-like they seem as they search desperately for their keys, wallets, and eyeglasses.

Although the dictionary definition of a senior moment is a "momentary lapse of memory, especially in older people"— hence the word "senior"— the term has come to mean any situation involving forgetfulness regardless of the sufferer's age. Just as seniors talk incessantly about things they can't remember, forgetful people in their thirties, forties, and fifties do the same.

Indeed, if you're a typical post-World War II "baby boomer" (just like the animatronics couple in the corner wearing their Sgt. Pepper's Lonely Hearts Club Band t-shirts), you probably use the term "senior moment" as much as, or even more than, your elders.

This is only fitting now that trend-spotting journalists have dubbed the tens of millions of baby boomers in the U.S. alone as "young seniors." Not regular seniors, mind you, because that would make boomers seem, well, old, and you don't feel old at all, do you? (Except, of course, when it's cold and damp and your children don't return your phone calls or e-mails.)

But I digress.

Let us now leave the Anteroom of Introduction and enter the room on our right — the right, for Heaven' sake, not the left! — which is commonly known as the...

ROOM OF TRANSIENCE

Although this room seems to be under construction to be finished later, it will never be changed, and for good reason.

Memory, you see, is usually temporary, just like this exhibit. Indeed, the time that you're most likely to forget information is right after you acquire it. This is known as "transience."

For example, if someone tells you a phone number just before you dial it, the number will probably fly out of your mind as soon as you're finished unless you make a concerted effort to memorize it.

The same holds true whenever you learn a new but less than earth-shattering fact. Let's say the information concerns those lemurs over there, which are busy exploring their half-finished habitat. If I tell you that lemurs are found naturally only on Madagascar and nearby islands, and that their weight ranges from one ounce to 22 pounds, it's not likely to stick in your memory if you don't have a reason to use it again.

Memories of experiences fade, too, as you can see in the adjacent display, which recreates an experiment using half-painted mannequins.

In this classic experiment, subjects were first asked to remember a dramatic event that occurred the day before: a simulated robbing of that suit-wearing experimenter standing in the corner. A day later, most subjects remembered significant details of the event, but after several months, only half were able to recall those same key details.

Our point is simple: Memory is usually impermanent, and forgetfulness is normal.

Although this may be troubling to most of you, imagine if the opposite were true. What would life be like if you could remember every instance in which you said or did something foolish, mean-spirited, or illegal? You might never get out of bed in the morning, and who could blame you?

As you ponder this sobering thought, let us next walk into the labyrinthine...

CHAMBER OF ABSENTMINDEDNESS

Absentmindedness usually occurs when you aren't paying enough attention to whatever you're doing. For example, you're not likely to remember where you left something if that information was never "encoded" properly in your memory in the first place.

Say you put something down while your mind was elsewhere. Or you forgot to look where you were going because you were worried about being late. Or you were asked to take care of something while you were struggling to remember another task, and so on and so forth.

The list of situations that can result in absentminded behavior is endless. (That's the same list you forgot to take with you this morning.)

Experts call this "divided attention." We call it "being distracted as usual."

Absentmindedness is a common phenomenon whenever we engage in routine activities without our full conscious awareness — as the actors shown here on the center screen are doing.

For example, how often have you found yourself driving without any memory of the previous ten minutes because you were on automatic pilot?

How often have you parked your car in a lot only to realize later that you never bothered to look around to see where you were?

How often have you found yourself unable to remember whether or not you locked the front door, turned off the faucet, mailed a letter, or promised to get a quart of milk?

The word is *absent*mindedness, remember, because your mind was absent at that moment. It's the price you pay for the ability to juggle a number of complex activities at the same time — activities such as thinking about lunch when you're supposed to be paying attention to me.

So, as we return to the main hallway, please make sure you at least pay special attention to the…

WALL OF BLOCKING

Notice that the opposite wall is covered with a dazzling, multi-colored rendering of thousands of names. This display is meant to visualize the problem of "blocking" names, an especially maddening form of forgetfulness.

Unlike a case of absentmindedness, the name you are trying to remember *was* properly encoded and stored in your long-term memory. And unlike memory lapses caused by transience, the information has not faded. It's there, all right. It's just out of reach.

This is the dreaded "on-the-tip-of-my-tongue" syndrome, which has been known to cause acute frustration, sudden bursts of anger, and even bouts of madness.

Proper names are blocked more often than others because they are seldom accompanied by a strong context clue — which is to say they are not well integrated with related associations, concepts, or knowledge that might possibly jog your memory.

See the name "Baker" on the wall over there? Unless Ms. Baker is actually a baker, you probably won't be able to hang her name on a key piece of related information — although you will be able to spend ten fruitless minutes trying to dredge up her name from your long-term memory while standing in front of her.

And now, finally, we come to the...

ATRIUM OF AGING

This rather old-fashioned, ramshackle room is always the last stop on our introductory tour. But before we go in, those of you who still have a spring in your step might want to wait outside to keep your illusions of eternal youth intact.

Fortunately, the snack bar and gift shop are located nearby.

As for the rest of us, let us press on.

Although everyone, young and old alike, can be forgetful, aging and memory loss do tend to go together like a horse and...

(Marriage? Claridge? Well, you know what I mean.)

Take a look at one of the "Mirrors of Maturity" on the far wall. If you gaze deeply into the one that's directly in front of you, you should be able to see yourself growing older, thanks to our absurdly expensive computer technology.

While you continue to fix your eyes on your own personal mirrors, let us march together through the decades:

First, you notice that beginning in your forties, you not only lose the ability to remember lyrics, but also find that recalling stories and past experiences with any degree of accuracy is more difficult.

Next, in your fifties, you find that just recalling a name is harder.

And by the time you reach your sixties and seventies, forgetfulness is a close companion, or at least an annoying, clingy acquaintance.

These days, alarming stories about Alzheimer's disease are increasing everybody's anxiety about memory lapses, often unnecessarily. This is not to dismiss the threat of Alzheimer's, which is real and growing as the population ages, but to counter the false connection between ordinary forgetfulness and the ravages of dementia.

The experts put it this way: If you forget where you put your keys, that's normal. If you forget that your keys open locks, then you should see a doctor as soon as possible.

Ironically, fretting too much about ordinary lapses of memory is counter-productive, not only because such lapses are inevitable, but also because worrying about them only makes things worse. There is considerable evidence that increased stress over forgetfulness can cause...even more forgetfulness.

For more scientific insights, why don't we gather around this giant model of a human brain with its 100 billion flashing neurons, trying hard not to get mesmerized by the lights and not faint.

On the whole, simple age-related memory impairment is not the result of disease but of normal changes in the brain, as you can see before you. The number and functioning of the synapses between neurons declines with age. And brain chemicals, called neurotransmitters, that facilitate communication between the neurons making memories possible, are not produced as readily.

And then there are the common ailments of aging that can also cause memory problems: high blood pressure, increased levels of cholesterol, excessive weight, having difficulty sleeping, and depression, among others.

(As a special service to visitors, our own Dr. Lenfloss is offering brief physical exams for those of you who are feeling a bit peaked. You can find him in the snack bar.)

The good news is that many popular beliefs about what happens to our brain as we age are either false or misleading.

Although it is true that most neuron growth occurs when we are young, we continue to create new ones throughout our lives. It is a process known as "neurogenesis." In fact, one of the hottest fields of research in neuroscience deals with the brain's "plasticity" — its ability to produce new nerve cells.

You can even see them growing in our model of the brain, although, admittedly, we have sped up the process a gazillion times.

In other words, thanks to neurogenesis, you are never too old to learn new tricks and form new memories. Even if you assume a net loss of thousands of neurons a day, it would take centuries before you lost more than a few percent of the total number. So breathe deeply and relax.

Well, what do you know? It looks as if it is finally time to enter the main exhibit hall and learn all about the Titans of Forgetfulness. We know that you're eager to get started, but before you go, we want to thank you from the bottom of our hearts for joining us here at the Senior Moments Hall of Fame.

And please, try not to get lost.

ANDRÉ-MARIE AMPÈRE

(1775–1836)

André-Marie Ampère, the great French physicist and mathematician who helped discover electromagnetism, will never be forgotten as long as the unit of measurement for electric current — the *ampere* or amp — continues to bear his name.

At least we hope so.

In 1809, Ampère became a professor of mathematics at the Polytechnic School in Paris, where many of his legendary memory lapses occurred. Well known for mulling over knotty scientific problems to the exclusion of all else, Ampère would often make notes with a piece of chalk wherever he happened to be. Any surface might be pressed into service, even the back of a horse-drawn carriage that was parked on the street. As Ampère was writing down a series of equations on one such carriage, he was shocked when his chalkboard drove away.

On Ampère's walks to the Polytechnic, anything could happen. One morning, as he was crossing the Pont des Arts over the Seine, he spied a curiously colored stone and stopped to pick it up. While he was examining it carefully, he suddenly realized he would be late for his lecture if he did not hurry.

After taking out his pocket watch to make sure of the time, Ampère quickened his pace across the bridge with the stone in one hand and the watch in the other. It was then that he absentmindedly put the stone in his pocket and tossed the watch into the river.

Dinner parties were problematic as well. Once, Ampère was busy enjoying himself at a dinner he had planned as a welcome for the noted physicist Leopold Nobili, who was visiting from Florence. While waiting for Nobili to arrive, Ampère regaled his guests with humorous stories and joined them in boisterous laughter. But a few moments later, he looked around the table and slumped in his chair, chagrined. When his colleagues asked him what was wrong, he confessed that he had forgotten to invite the guest of honor.

During a routine visit to a friend's house, he typically wandered off before the evening meal. When it was time to sit down and eat, his host sent his servants off to fetch the missing professor, as usual. But after searching all the obvious places where Ampère might be, the servants were forced to admit defeat, and the remaining company had no choice but to continue without him.

Finally, when a servant went to retrieve an extra table for dessert, he found Ampère in a small storeroom, reading a book. The scientist had been so preoccupied, he not only forgot dinner, but also squeezed himself into a corner in such an unnatural position for such a long time that his legs cramped and could no longer support him.

Unable to stand on his own, he had to be carried to the dinner table, at which point he was gently placed in his chair, having missed dinner entirely (except for dessert, of course). Ampère was so accustomed to such bouts of absentmindedness, however, that he gamely entered the conversation as if nothing odd had happened.

And perhaps nothing odd *had* happened, at least in Ampère's mind. This, after all, was a man who, when invited to dine with Napoleon, the most powerful man in the world, forgot to show up.

LUDWIG VAN BEETHOVEN

(1770–1827)

The great German composer Beethoven prided himself on his keen memory. "I carry my thoughts about me for a long time before I write them down," he declared. "Meanwhile my memory is so tenacious that I am sure never to forget, not even in years, a theme that has once occurred to me."

Of course, he was referring to his musical memory, you understand. As for his other powers of recall, well, "tenacious" is hardly the word one would use.

For example, when Beethoven went to a restaurant for dinner one evening, he soon forgot why he was there. When a waiter repeatedly asked him what he wanted to order, Beethoven was so preoccupied (perhaps with a theme that had once occurred to him), he waved the man away.

Finally, after more than an hour, the composer snapped out of his reverie and called over the waiter. Assuming that he must have eaten — or why else was he still there? — Beethoven asked for the check.

This sort of behavior was quite familiar to his friends. One morning, a fellow composer and pianist, Ignaz Moscheles, went to visit Beethoven in his Vienna apartment, only to find him still in bed. This time the usually grumpy genius was in exceptionally good humor. He greeted Moscheles warmly, jumped out of bed, pulled back the curtains, and stood standing at the window overlooking the street, admiring the view. When he noticed some boys staring up at him, pointing and laughing, the composer complained, "Those damned boys! What do they want?"

It wasn't until Moscheles gestured to his friend's midsection that Beethoven looked down and realized he was naked.

Beethoven was especially absentminded while composing. To keep his mind sharp, he would first dip his head in cold water and then pour more water on his hands, one pitcher after another, until his clothes were sopping wet. Next, he would pace about the room humming to himself before he sat down to write.

None of his visitors dared to interrupt him during the ritual, although it might have been better if they had. Beethoven's landlords, who lived below him, were furious when water invariably dripped through the ceiling. No wonder the composer moved so often.

But perhaps Beethoven's most impressive bout of absentmindedness came at the premiere of one of his piano concertos, when he forgot he was supposed to be the soloist, and nothing more. Instead, seized by excitement, he jumped up from his piano and began to conduct, throwing out his arms so wildly that he knocked over two lamps that were lighting his music stand. With the ensuing crash, Beethoven lost his concentration and abruptly stopped the orchestra, insisting that the musicians start over.

The actual conductor, whose position Beethoven had just usurped, began to fear that the composer might leap up again and cause even more havoc. So he ordered two boys who were backstage to stand next to the piano and hold up the lamps, gripping them as tightly as they could.

However, when one of the boys stepped closer to the piano to better follow the score, Beethoven flung out his left hand to punctuate the music and slapped the poor lad in the face. The audience burst out laughing, enraging the composer. Beethoven then struck the piano keys so hard, he broke six strings, which is almost as impressive as forgetting that you're the soloist and not the conductor at the premiere of your own composition.

ERMA BOMBECK

(1927–1996)

If laughing at your own senior moments is good therapy, then getting other people to laugh at them while being paid handsomely is even better.

Erma Bombeck, the popular humorist, wrote a newspaper column and 15 books describing the ups and downs of middle age in a suburban household. You can sum up her appeal with one of her classic lines: "Since 40 I can't remember a thing, including the fact that I reached 40."

Millions of readers knew that if anyone could empathize with their daily battle against the aggravations of absentmindedness, it was Erma Bombeck. By making her senior moments public, she transformed them from disturbing embarrassments suffered alone to routine glitches that everyone shared sooner or later.

"In some little restaurant, somewhere in the city," she wrote, "my very best friend, what's-her-name, is throwing down bread sticks waiting for me to join her for lunch." (In this case, Bombeck had lost the note she wrote to remind herself of the appointment.)

The subject of many Bombeck columns was forgetting where she put important items, such as the household folder labeled IMPORTANT PAPERS! (As everyone knows, if you use the word "important" on any folder, envelope, or box, and then capitalize it for good measure, you will never find the papers when you need them most.)

Bombeck's husband was incredulous. Without that folder, they couldn't put their hands on their car registration, life insurance policy, the deed to their house, or their will. But all was not lost (so to speak). After a great deal of effort, the papers were found, one by one.

In a true testament to the power of absentmindedness, the car registration was being used as a bookmark in a novel that hadn't been picked up in years. The life insurance policy was in Bombeck's husband's shirt drawer. The deed to the house was in the attic in a box labeled "maternity clothes." And the will was in a pocket of a suit jacket her husband had worn to their lawyer's office on the day the will was drawn up.

As for the folder marked IMPORTANT PAPERS, it was in the sewing machine drawer — and didn't contain a single important paper.

Bombeck also wrote eloquently about the Curse of the Missing Keys (somewhat like the Curse of the Missing Tools, only without the tools). She frequently compared keys to umbrellas: You never think about them until you need them and can't find them.

Over the years, she accidentally mailed keys in letters, dropped them in bowls in obscure corners of the house, and left them outside, hanging in the lock of her front door.

Looking on the bright side, she did learn some useful new skills. "Since last February I have broken into my house 38 times," she wrote proudly.

Children also provided endless opportunities for senior moments, as any parent can attest. For the rest of your life, complained Bombeck, people expect you to remember your children's names and ages instantly, upon demand, as if it were a test of some sort — a test you're bound to fail. And to think that these people would never even give you the chance to count on your fingers, or make a phone call!

There is no end to the indignities of a bad memory. As Bombeck wrote in a 1987 column, "One of my sons who is…let's just say he is older today than he was 10 years ago…accuses me of telling the wrong stories about the wrong kid. I thought he was the one who said the cute things that I used to submit to *Reader's Digest*, but it turns out it was his brother."

Her fitting conclusion? "Whatever…"

ALEXANDER BORODIN

(1833–1887)

Born in St. Petersburg, Alexander Borodin was a composer, chemist, researcher, professor, military surgeon, physician, and champion of women's rights. No wonder he was so easily distracted.

Best known today for his symphonies and string quartets, Borodin was so busy with his other, non-musical commitments that he once protested to his friends that he was merely a "Sunday composer."

After he began one of his most famous works, the opera *Prince Igor*, he put it aside, only to forget that he had written the music for an opera, and used it for a symphony instead.

Over the years, he would write an aria for *Prince Igor* from time to time, always putting it aside and absent-mindedly moving on, to one thing or another. In fact, the opera wasn't finished until his fellow Russian composer Rimsky-Korsakov took up the challenge — three years after Borodin's death.

Like many Titans of Forgetfulness, the composer-chemist-professor-physician had trouble keeping his meals straight. On some days, he would eat two soft-boiled eggs and nothing else, while on others he would eat two full dinners, having forgotten about the first when he sat down for the second.

Of course, some senior moments are more embarrassing than others. As a reserve officer in the Russian Army, he was required to participate in the occasional full dress parade. And so one day he put on his military jacket, which was splendidly adorned with rows of medals, then carefully adjusted his plumed helmet, and marched out of his house en route to the ceremony without his pants on.

Sometimes, a senior moment is a logical extension of your true feelings, which you're expected to keep to yourself — unless you forgot. Consider the time Borodin was asked to testify in court as an expert witness in a case involving two young composers who accused each other of plagiarism. After their respective (and strangely familiar) compositions were played, Borodin was asked by the judge to give his learned opinion. Was it the first young composer who stole from the second or vice versa?

Borodin's expert opinion? Both of them had stolen from his friend Mussorgsky.

WILLIAM LISLE BOWLES

(1762–1850)

Reverend William Lisle Bowles was an admired clergyman, a kind and gentle soul, a talented if minor poet, and a reliable friend. But according to those who knew him best, his most distinguishing characteristic was his unreliable memory.

One evening, at a dinner party, he kept his guests waiting for an unusually long time. When Mrs. Bowles went upstairs to find out what was keeping her husband, she found him barefoot in their bedroom, hunting everywhere for a missing silk stocking, without which he wouldn't be fully dressed and couldn't join his guests.

After beginning her own lengthy search, Mrs. Bowles finally saved her husband from further embarrassment by noticing that he had put both stockings on the same leg.

Unlike some other Titans of Forgetfulness, Bowles was aware that his memory was, um, a bit faulty. As he admitted to a friend, "I never had but one watch, and I lost it the very first day I wore it."

Mrs. Bowles then added in a whisper, "And if he got another one today, he would lose it just as quickly."

The minister's neighbors, who saw his forgetfulness as more of an endearing trait than a fault, swore that, once, when Bowles' own house was pointed out to him, he couldn't remember who lived there.

Each morning, it was Bowles habit to ride on a local toll road, which required him to pay the gatekeeper two pence for the privilege of taking his horse through. But one day, when he passed through the gate on foot, he handed the gatekeeper the usual sum anyway.

When the man asked him what the money was for, Bowles replied in surprise, "For my horse, of course."

"But sir, you have no horse!" the puzzled gatekeeper exclaimed.

Bowles, in turn, looked around in confusion and asked, "Oh, am I walking?"

His mind often worked in mysterious ways. When Bowles gave a parishioner a Bible as a birthday present, she asked him to write an inscription. Pleased to oblige, he signed it, "From the author."

Not everyone was charmed by Bowles' senior moments. Madame de Staël, the famous French author who presided over a highly popular salon in Paris, was definitely one. When she decided to visit England, she expressed a wish to meet "Mr. Bowles the poet," having admired his sonnets.

Something was bound to go wrong, and did. While Bowles was riding to meet de Staël at a party given by Lord Lansdowne in her honor, he fell from his horse and sprained his shoulder. But even though he was in considerable pain, he pressed on.

When the clergyman finally arrived at the party, he was introduced to the formidable Frenchwoman. Lord Lansdowne then alluded to the accident as a sign of Bowles' eagerness to meet de Staël.

Unfortunately for a senior moment sufferer, there is many a slip 'twixt brain and lip.

When Madame de Staël thanked Bowles for making the effort to see her, injured as he was, he replied, "Oh M'am, say no more about it, for I would have done a great deal more to see such a great curiosity."

De Staël was so offended by his absentminded choice of words — a curiosity? like an animal in a zoo? c'est ignoble! — she never forgot it for years to come, whereas Reverend Bowles was unable to recall it.

MARLON BRANDO

(1924–2004)

Many people in the Senior Moments Hall of Fame have been described as larger than life, but few were as large as Marlon Brando — in talent, eccentricity, self-indulgence, appetite, and eventually, forgetfulness.

Brando was notoriously cavalier about blowing his lines. During the production of *The Island of Dr. Moreau*, director John Frankenheimer had to rig the actor with a small radio receiver, which he placed in Brando's ear in order to feed him dialogue. But the receiver also picked up police transmissions. Brando was in the middle of an important scene when he delivered one of cinema's immortal lines: "There's a robbery at Woolworths!"

Then there was the time Brando was shooting a scene in a remake of *Mutiny on the Bounty*. It was the scene in which his character, Fletcher Christian, had just been burned. When the method actor learned that burn victims can feel as if they are freezing, he ordered a bed of cracked ice he could lie on just before the cameras rolled.

Trembling uncontrollably, he announced he was finally ready to film the scene. He staggered to his feet from the bed of ice, got into position, opened his mouth to deliver his lines...and discovered that he couldn't recall a single word — this during a production that was already plagued by costly delays. Forced to improvise, John Frankenheimer instructed a crewmember to write Brando's dialogue on the forehead of another actor, who was standing opposite the star.

When Brando was both the leading man and the director for the same film, anything could happen. On the set of *One-Eyed Jacks*, he spent days waiting for the perfect ocean background before shooting a scene on a beach. The waves had to be just right, he insisted — high, but not too high, with enough white foam to serve as a contrast to the deep blue of the Pacific.

As Brando looked through his viewfinder hour after hour, he kept complaining that the waves seemed so puny, totally unsuitable for such a dramatic scene. The crew's agony finally ended only when Brando realized he was looking at the waves through the wrong end of the viewfinder.

ANTON BRUCKNER

(1824–1896)

An especially unfortunate memory lapse of the Austrian composer Anton Bruckner was immortalized by another great Austrian composer, his good friend Gustav Mahler.

After a lengthy illness, Bruckner was ordered by his doctor to take a daily bath. "Loathe to waste time," recalled Mahler, "[Anton] would take music paper and compose in the tub."

One day, while absorbed in his work, Bruckner was interrupted by a pupil's mother, who was knocking on his front door.

"Come in!" Bruckner called out without a moment's thought.

Mahler described what happened next: "Imagine her consternation on entering the apartment, to see Bruckner's portly person in the bathtub, naked as the good Lord had fashioned him. As she stood there transfixed, Bruckner politely got up and walked over, dripping wet, to greet her. Only her shriek and hasty exit made the poor man aware of his condition."

The senior moments of a fully clothed Bruckner could be just as memorable. For a rehearsal by the Vienna Philharmonic Orchestra of one of his symphonies, the composer was invited to conduct. After Bruckner duly arrived at the concert hall and took his place on the conductor's platform, he stood motionless for several minutes, beaming at the musicians without lifting his baton.

Finally, the orchestra's music director, Arnold Rosé, said gently, "We are quite ready, Herr Bruckner. Do begin."

"Oh no," replied the composer. "After you, gentlemen!"

Now you might think that a great composer engaged in such a serious endeavor as the performance of his own work would be utterly focused, and thus immune to a senior moment. But you would be wrong.

Once, when another conductor of the Vienna Philharmonic, Hans Richter, was rehearsing a new work by

Bruckner, he looked over at the composer and asked, "F or F sharp?"

Startled, Bruckner leaped to his feet and blurted out, "Whichever you like!"

Richter was a great admirer of Bruckner as a composer and as a gentle and generous man, but even he could not deny that his good friend often forgot what sort of behavior was appropriate in certain situations. After an especially satisfying rehearsal of Bruckner's Fourth Symphony, the delighted composer actually tipped the conductor, pressing a coin into his hand.

Richter might have been startled, but he certainly was not offended. He knew Bruckner too well for that. Instead, he attached the coin to his watch chain and wore it for the rest of his life.

There are some senior moments that warm the heart....

G. K. CHESTERTON

(1874–1936)

Gilbert Keith Chesterton wrote some 80 books, 200 short stories, 200 poems, 4000 essays, and a handful of plays. He was a journalist, literary critic, social critic, historian, Catholic theologian, and public debater. Not surprisingly, he was often so preoccupied that he couldn't remember where he was going or what he was supposed to do when he got there.

Chesterton's senior moments were legendary. One evening, he borrowed a corkscrew from his neighbor, but upon returning to his house, discovered that his key no longer worked. It was only after repeated attempts to unlock his front door that he realized that the "key" was actually the corkscrew.

Chesterton was always thinking over a story or essay while walking about London, and as a result, often became hopelessly lost. Sometimes he would even find himself standing in the middle of a road as the traffic veered around him. He would then head for the nearest pay phone and call his wife for directions on how to get back.

Chesterton could get lost anywhere. Once, while on a lecture tour, he sent his wife the following telegram: "Am in Birmingham. Where ought I to be?"

She promptly wired back: "Home."

As for Chesterton's writing, much of it was done in train stations — after he missed a train. Indeed, there was something about trains and train stations that seemed to scramble his memory. One morning, when he went up to a ticket window, he asked the agent for a cup of coffee. After realizing his mistake, he walked into the station restaurant to wait and asked the waiter for a train ticket.

Confusion over clothing also added to his legend. Chesterton was easily identified by his impressive girth, voluminous cloak, and broad-brimmed hat. But this was not an eccentric fashion statement, as many believed, but an attempt by his exasperated wife to protect him from ridicule.

In situations where wearing the right clothes was especially important, Chesterton might turn up in a suit and coat he absentmindedly had borrowed from a friend who was half his size, with only his cloak concealing the evidence.

His wife must have been an extremely patient woman. Certainly she must have known what was she getting herself into from the very beginning of their marriage. After all, on the way to the church for his wedding, Chesterton stopped for a glass of milk at the local dairy and bought a revolver at the gunsmith's shop, a purchase he had planned to make for some time. And what better time to do it than on one's wedding day?

Then he nearly sabotaged the honeymoon by losing their luggage.

On the other hand, Chesterton was always the first to make fun of his unreliable memory. As he wrote to a friend, "On rising this morning, I carefully washed my boots in hot water and put boot polish on my face, poured coffee on my sardines, and put my hat on the fire to boil. These activities will give you some idea of my state of mind."

PAUL DIRAC

(1902–1984)

The inspiring example of Paul Dirac stands as proof that a genius can win a Nobel Prize for Physics for groundbreaking work on atomic theory and yet still forget the name of his new wife.

It happened the day after his marriage to the sister of his old friend, Eugene Wigner, the Hungarian theoretical physicist. When another one of his friends, who didn't know about the wedding, showed up unannounced on Dirac's doorstep, an attractive woman he had never met before graciously served him tea and biscuits.

"How do you do?" the friend asked politely, trying desperately to figure out who the woman might possibly be. It was only then that Dirac remembered his manners. "Oh, I'm sorry, I forgot to introduce you. This is," he began to say while gesturing at his wife. "This is... Wigner's sister."

Dirac's absentmindedness was on display every day in the classroom. After the physicist wrote an equation on the blackboard during one lecture, a student raised his hand and said plaintively, "Professor Dirac, I don't understand Equation Two."

When Dirac continued writing as if the student had not spoken, the young man raised his hand again, still hoping for an explanation.

"Professor, I just don't understand the equation," he pleaded.

Again, Dirac continued writing with his back to the class.

Finally, a second (and rather brave) student spoke up, pointing to the first student: "Professor, I think he asked you a question."

Only then did Dirac realize that some kind of reaction was called for. He stopped writing, turned around, and said, "Oh, I thought he was making a statement."

During his most creative years, Dirac avoided nearly all social contact. He worked six days a week, and on Sundays took a long walk in the country. He was uninterested in possessions and wore the same overcoat for 50 years.

Even those who knew him best admitted they often had no idea what was going on in his mind. As Albert Einstein said of him, "This balancing on the dizzying path between genius and madness is awful."

On the other hand, it's only fair to point out that Dirac did, in fact, remember that his new wife's name was Margit after only a few (very long) minutes.

ROBERT DOLE

(1923–)

Robert Dole, the former Republican senator from Kansas, is the only person in the history of the United States to be a major party's nominee for both President and Vice President and then lose both elections. Perhaps this explains why his mind wandered from time to time.

For example, shortly after his wife Elizabeth made a decision to campaign for the presidency, Dole seems to have forgotten all about it. He told a reporter that he would be contributing money to one of his wife's chief opponents, his old friend John McCain.

Losing his train of thought was a Bob Dole specialty. Attempting to explain the difficulty faced by politicians who were intent on preserving the separation between public and private life, he declared, "You read what Disraeli had to say...."

So far so good, but then he added, "I don't remember what he said. He said something."

And finally finished up with, "He's no longer with us."

Disraeli died in 1881.

On other occasions, the absentminded Dole would wander haplessly through a verbal maze from which there was no escape.

It was he who once said, "Life is very important to Americans."

And then there was this classic line: "The internet is a great way...to get on the net."

But the favorite of most senior moment aficionados was the following: "We know smoking tobacco is not good for kids, but a lot of other things are not good. Drinking is not good. Some would say milk is not good."

To this day no one is sure quite what he meant, perhaps not even Dole himself.

When he became the Senate Majority Leader of the newly triumphant Republicans in 1995, the connection between mind and mouth was already terribly frayed.

Referring to the members of his own party (and no doubt forgetting that he would be dealing with them repeatedly and at great length), Dole told reporters, "If we had known we were gong to win control of the Senate, we'd have run better candidates."

ALBERT EINSTEIN

(1879–1955)

To be remembered by the public long after one has passed away is rare, but to be remembered as both the archetypal genius of modern times, smarter than anyone else, and the archetypal absentminded professor, more forgetful than anyone else...well, *that* is truly extraordinary.

When it comes to the genius who gave us the General and Special Theories of Relativity, we can always mumble $E = MC^2$ (energy equals mass times the speed of light squared) and leave it at that. Then we can concentrate on our true field of expertise, which is $AA = DSM^2$ (acute absentmindedness equals the number of distractions times the number of senior moments squared).

Einstein could get so caught up in mulling over scientific ideas that he would overlook everything else. When he was working out his General Theory of Relativity, he often forgot to sleep or eat. Once, while he was living in Switzerland, his friends bought him a full tin of caviar for his twenty-fourth birthday. He was so engrossed in a discussion of inertia that he gobbled down the entire (and extremely expensive) tin in one sitting without even noticing (or sharing).

In 1930, when he traveled to the United States from Berlin, he recorded the details of his trip. The Einstein Archive sums up an excerpt from his travel diary this way: "The page depicted here describes the hectic departure of Einstein and his wife Elsa from the railway station in Berlin, 30 November 1930. First he loses his wife, finds her again, and then he loses the tickets and finds them as well. Thus began Einstein's second trip to the U.S."

According to his cousin, the economist Norbert Einstein, Albert's wife Elsa once asked Norbert to take Albert to a special meeting of a physics society in Berlin, a meeting at which Albert was the guest of honor.

"He came into the room in a tacky tuxedo and dirty shirt," Norbert recalled. "Elsa sent him back to the bedroom to put on a clean shirt."

When Einstein failed to return, Norbert and Elsa went to the bedroom to fetch him. He was propped up in bed, undressed, reading Spinoza. He had forgotten all about the meeting.

When Einstein moved to Princeton, New Jersey, in 1932 to take up residence at the Institute for Advanced Study, his senior moments seemed to multiply.

Historian James R. Blackwood, the author of *Einstein in the Rear-view Mirror*, lived next door to Albert and Elsa. He recalled that once, when Einstein's mother was sitting in the living room talking with Elsa, "Einstein was in the music room improvising on the piano. The music stopped and Einstein came past them, hair straying in all directions, no shirt or undershirt on, trousers sadly drooping and, I think, barefoot. He walked past them as if in a trance."

There was no sense of embarrassment or recognition of his mother's presence. "He just drifted past and walked upstairs," wrote Blackwood, "while a chagrined Mrs. Einstein clasped her hands and said, 'Oh, Albertle!'"

One day, someone called the Advanced Institute and asked to speak to a particular dean. When the dean's secretary said that he wasn't available, the caller asked hesitatingly for Einstein's home address. The secretary replied that she couldn't give out personal information to just anyone. That's when the caller's voice dropped to an embarrassed whisper. "*I* am Dr. Einstein," he explained.

He had taken a long walk, gotten lost, and then forgot where his house was.

Another time, Einstein and an assistant were searching his office for a paper clip. When they finally found one, it was too mangled to use, so another search began — this time to find a tool that could straighten the clip.

As they looked around the office again, they came upon...a large box of paper clips. Success at last! Or so you might think. But instead of simply taking out a new clip and using it as it was meant to be used, Einstein selected a clip to shape into a tool that could straighten out the old, twisted clip, having completely forgotten the point of the original search.

Other senior moments involved Einstein's role as a public figure. His fame in the United States was such that he was in great demand as a speaker. But when he received a $1,500 check from the Rockefeller Foundation as an honorarium, he used it as a bookmark for months.

Trying to keep the Foundation's records in order, an accountant eventually noticed that Einstein's check had never been cashed, so he sent another one to the physicist. But Einstein, having forgotten all about the first one, enclosed the check in an envelope and sent it right back, accompanied by a note asking, "What's this for?"

As a world celebrity, Einstein was as recognizable as any movie star and thus irresistible to photographers. There is a famous picture that shows him thoughtfully rubbing his chin as if he were pondering the mysteries of the universe. But according to the photographer, Ernest Haas, he had just asked Einstein where on the shelf behind him he had placed a particular book. In other words, the mysteries of the universe were actually the mysteries of a bad memory.

Although everybody knew of Einstein, few were close to him. He seemed remote at social gatherings and was frequently in a vague dreamy mood when in the company of others, seemingly unaware of what was going on around him.

He was once traveling on a train from Princeton when the conductor came down the aisle, punching the tickets of the passengers. When he came to Einstein, the physicist reached in his vest pocket, but could not find his ticket. He reached into his pants pockets, but it wasn't there either. Next, he looked in his briefcase, but again, he could not find it. Then he looked all around the seat beside him. Nothing.

Finally, the conductor took pity on him. Trying to be reassuring, he said, "Dr. Einstein, I know who you are.

We all know who you are. I'm sure you bought a ticket. Don't worry about it."

Einstein nodded appreciatively.

The conductor continued down the aisle, punching tickets. But as he was about to move on to the next car, he turned around and saw Einstein down on his hands and knees looking under his seat for his ticket. Appalled, the conductor rushed back to reassure him again.

"Dr. Einstein, Dr. Einstein, don't worry!" he insisted. "I know who you are. It's no problem. You don't need a ticket. I'm sure you bought one."

Einstein looked at the conductor closely and then said, 'Young man, I, too, know who I am. What I don't know is where I am going."

Reacting to repeated discussions of what a fine president of Israel his cousin Albert would make, Norbert Einstein commented wryly, "He lived out there in the universe. He would have made a fine president of the universe. But not of any place on Earth."

GEORGE ELIOT

(1819–1880)

Mary Ann Evans, the brilliant English novelist who wrote under the name George Eliot, had the intense focus necessary to write such staples of school reading lists everywhere as *Silas Marner* and *Middlemarch*. And yet, when it came to everyday matters, she could be remarkably fuzzy.

One night, a visitor, the artist Edward Burne-Jones, asked Eliot for directions to the local station so he could return home on the last train. Eliot smiled, waved vaguely to the right, and told him that if he just kept going in that direction he was sure to find the station.

Before Burne-Jones had a chance to ask for a few more details (that she wouldn't have remembered anyway), Eliot bid him goodnight and shut the door firmly behind him. And so he had no choice but to stumble blindly down the unlit drive.

When he reached the lane that ran in front of the house, he dutifully turned to the right.

That's when his troubles began.

His first obstacle was an unexpected fence, which he was forced to climb over. Then, when he made it to the other side, he tripped and rolled down a 30-foot hill.

His body badly bruised by rocks, and his clothes torn to ribbons by branches and brambles, he finally arrived at the station, glad to be alive.

George Eliot had been correct, after all; the station was to the right — in a general sort of way.

Perhaps her absentmindedness was due in part to the over-solicitous devotion of her longtime partner, George Henry Lewes.

One day in London, the same unfortunate Edward Burne-Jones (not having learned his lesson) came across Eliot again, this time standing alone. After they walked together a short distance, chatting about this and that, Lewes rushed up to them in a panic. "My God!" he said to Eliot. "You are here!"

When she agreed that, indeed, she was "here," Lewes exclaimed, "But I left you there," pointing to a spot ten yards away. That she would have walked the entire distance without Lewes escorting her horrified him no end.

With someone like Lewes around, perhaps you, too, might delegate the task of remembering pesky details like directions and appointments so you didn't have to bother with them, keeping your mind free of annoying clutter.

PAUL ERDÖS

(1913–1996)

The great 20th century Hungarian mathematician Paul Erdös never forgot a number, including the telephone numbers of hundreds of colleagues. It was just their first names he couldn't recall.

Granted, Erdös had a lot on his mind. He published more papers than any other mathematician in history. He also wrote 1500 letters a year, almost all concerning mathematical problems. A typical Erdös letter began this way: "I am in Austria. Tomorrow I leave for Hungary. Let k be the largest integer…"

His absentmindedness was legendary. Totally uninterested in money and possessions, Erdös traveled constantly from conference to conference and university to university, relying on the kindness of friends for meals and lodging.

His hosts knew him well enough to prepare for almost anything. Once, a colleague discovered Erdös in his kitchen in the middle of the night. Alarmingly, the mathematician was standing in a pool of what looked like blood. On a counter nearby was a large carving knife, coated with the same red liquid.

Fearing the worst, the colleague rushed to Erdös's side. But the mathematician was fine, if a little perplexed. He had simply wandered into the kitchen looking for something to drink. When he opened the refrigerator, he found a carton of tomato juice and decided to pour himself a glass. But he had forgotten the customary way to open a carton of juice, so he picked up the carving knife and stabbed it repeatedly.

If this sounds farfetched, consider the following:

At many a dinner the ever-curious mathematician would point to a dish of food and ask his hosts what it was and how it was prepared. Now this would make perfect sense if the dish were exotic. But what if Erdös had eaten it many times before and still couldn't remember its name or recall any explanation of how it was cooked?

The dish in question was a bowl of rice.

Andrew Vázsonyi, who was a 14 year-old mathematics prodigy when he first met Erdös in Budapest, remembered every detail of another singular Erdös senior moment, even though it occurred decades before.

At the time, Vázsonyi was living in a house in Manhattan Beach, California, waiting for his old friend to return from a short walk on the esplanade out front. Erdös hadn't been gone for more than ten minutes when the telephone rang. A woman on the line explained that there was a gentleman at her door who had just told her he was visiting the Vázsonyi family, but had gotten lost and, unfortunately, couldn't remember their address or how to find his way back.

Vázsonyi told the woman, "Please tell him to stand on the esplanade and look north, and he will see me waving."

Vázsonyi dutifully walked out his door and sure enough, there was Erdös just a few blocks away.

"How he could have gotten lost on the esplanade, which runs in a straight line with no forks, I will never know," Vázsonyi marveled.

If you asked Erdös about number theory, approximation theory, probability theory, or any other mathematical theory, he could discuss it in great detail without hesitation. After all, he had 15 honorary doctorates and was elected to scientific academies in eight countries.

You just couldn't ask him about anything else.

GERALD FORD

(1913–2006)

He was truly the "accidental President," as he was once widely known.

Gerald Ford, a long-time Michigan congressman and Republican Minority Leader, was appointed to the vice presidency by Richard Nixon in 1973 after Spiro Agnew, the man who had been elected vice president in 1972, resigned in disgrace. Then, a year later, it was Nixon's turn to resign in disgrace. Suddenly Ford was elevated to the presidency of the world's most powerful nation, much to his and everyone else's surprise.

Such an improbable sequence of events would probably discombobulate anyone, but Ford didn't help matters when his mind went blank at the most inopportune times, or when he tripped and fell in public while the cameras were rolling. And so it was that the man who had been a college football star and graduated from Yale Law School became an object of mockery.

As a supporter of the School Lunch Bill, Ford once declared, "I strongly support the feeding of children."

As a big sports fan, he explained that he watched "a lot of baseball on the radio."

As a student of history, he scolded, "If Lincoln was alive today, he'd roll over in his grave."

As a veteran giver of speeches, he called Mesa College in Colorado, "Meesa College," and then correcting himself, "Messa College."

As an amateur philosopher, he reflected aloud, "Things are more like they are now than they have ever been before."

It was just as well that Ford's priceless senior moments had Americans chuckling during a time of economic and political turmoil. After Jimmy Carter got in trouble for admitting in an interview that, although he had always been faithful to his wife, he still lusted in his heart, it was Ford who said innocently, "I've only lusted after two women in my life — my wife Betty and my mother Mom."

Ford's absentminded comments could seem other-worldly in their bewildering incoherence. In November 1974, he explained to a head-scratching audience, "You know we have three great branches of this government of ours. We have a strong President, supposedly in the White House. We have a strong Congress, supposedly in the legislative branch. And we have a strong Supreme Court, supposedly heading the judiciary system."

Ford was in the throes of absentmindedness on a political trip to the West Coast when he stopped at Utah State University to see his son Jack, who was an under-graduate at the time. When Ford arrived on campus, he first had to wade through a large group of students who wanted to meet him. One of the students was Jack, who smiled to himself when his father automatically shook his hand without the slightest glimmer of recognition and then kept moving through the crowd on his way to see... Jack.

But perhaps the most impressive senior moment of Gerald Ford's political career came in a debate with Jimmy Carter during the 1976 presidential campaign. While answering a question about the Soviet Union and its sphere of influence, he stated, "There is no Soviet domination of Eastern Europe, and there never will be under the Ford administration."

Surely the President had misheard the question, said the New York Times reporter who had asked him about Romania and was now offering him an honorable way out. Unfortunately, Ford took this as a splendid opportunity to show just how lost he could get in his own mind:

"I don't believe, Mr. Frankel, that the Romanians consider themselves dominated by the Soviet Union. I don't believe that the Poles consider themselves dominated by the Soviet Union. Each of these countries is independent, autonomous. It has its own territorial integrity and the United States does not concede that those countries are under the domination of the Soviet Union."

A few days later he tried to clarify his position, which he realized had come out terribly wrong: "We are going to make certain to the best of our ability that any allegation of domination is not a fact," he stated.

After this final attempt, he wisely gave up with the understatement of the year: "I did not express myself clearly, I admit."

By then, however, Ford had been defeated by Jimmy Carter, whose own senior moments weren't nearly as amusing.

JOHN GIELGUD

(1904–2000)

Sir John Gielgud was famous for his extraordinary voice, which Alec Guinness once described as a "silver trumpet muffled in silk." He was also one of just a handful of performers to win an Oscar, Emmy, Grammy, and Tony Award. And yet Gielgud's theatrical gifts, great as they were, could not match his mastery of the senior moment.

This was obvious from the very beginning of his illustrious career. In 1932, while still an undergraduate at Oxford University, he played Romeo in a Dramatic Society production along with such future luminaries as Peggy Ashcroft in the role of Juliet and Edith Evans as the Nurse.

The first performance was rather bumpy, and by the final curtain, Gielgud was a nervous wreck. Although he had rehearsed a number of effusive compliments for Evans and Ashcroft, when he finally faced the audience at the end of the play, his mind went blank and he wound up thanking his two leading ladies, "the like of whom I hope I shall never meet again."

Gielgud's flamboyant forgetfulness remained undiminished through the years. When he visited Richard Burton backstage after the latter's debut performance as Hamlet in 1953, he found Burton in a miserable state. He was suffering from a bad cold that had clearly affected his performance, which was rather flat. Said Gielgud sympathetically, "I'll look in and see you again when you're better."

It was only after Burton flinched that Gielgud realized his mistake and added quickly, "I mean in health, of course."

After a performance of his own one evening, Gielgud was visited in his dressing room by a man who wished to offer his compliments, just as Gielgud had meant to do with Burton. Pleased that he recognized the visitor's face, Gielgud greeted him with pleasure. "I used to know your son," he said. "We were at school together!"

But the actor's memory had betrayed him again. "I don't have a son," the man replied sourly. "*I* was at school with you."

Always the entertainer, Gielgud was known to amuse his friends by mocking his own senior moments. "When Clement Attlee was prime minister," he once related, "I was asked to meet him at Stratford-upon-Avon at a supper at the Falcon Hotel after he attended a performance I was not in myself. I sat next to his daughter, and the conversation turned on where we lived. 'I have a very convenient home in Westminster,' I remarked. 'So easy to walk to the theatre. And where do you live?'"

Miss Attlee looked distinctly surprised, and then replied coldly, as if Gielgud had meant to make fun of her, "Number 10 Downing Street."

One of Sir John's most renowned senior moments occurred at the final dress rehearsal of a production of *Don Giovanni*. Gielgud was serving as director, a role that never really suited him. The opera was well under way when he noticed that members of the chorus were wandering about the stage, trying to find their places, which Gielgud had forgotten to show them.

He rose from his seat without thinking and rushed down to the front of the hall to tell them what to do. But as the orchestra played on relentlessly, he could not be heard. Suddenly, his voice rose above the din: "Oh, do stop that awful music!" he wailed.

He was also well known for forgetting to whom he was talking. While having lunch with actress Athene Seyler one afternoon, Gielgud bemoaned his fate. "These days I seem to spend all my time in the company of these old bags of the screen," he complained. "Monday, Fay Compton. Tuesday, Sybil Thorndike. Wednesday, Athene Seyler."

He stopped short when he saw the expression on Seyler's face, and added quickly, "Of course, I don't mean you, Athene!"

Fortunately, at least for us, Gielgud was always able to top himself, even when it seemed he already had reached the pinnacle of forgetfulness. When an actor friend was describing a colleague of both men as a "frightful curmudgeon, really impossible," with a chip on his shoulder because of his faltering career, Gielgud's reply was priceless. "Yes," he said, "but you're a failure, and you haven't got a chip on your shoulder."

SAMUEL GOLDWYN

(1882–1974)

In his long Hollywood career, studio chief Samuel Goldwyn earned a stellar reputation for picking winners (hence his star on the Hollywood Walk of Fame) and for losing the meaning of a statement somewhere between the beginning and the end. Not that Goldwyn would ever admit it. As he famously declared when he was urged to change his mind about a script, "I'm willing to admit that I may not always be right, but I am never wrong!"

It was once suggested that arbitration was the best way to settle a heated dispute between Goldwyn and another Hollywood mogul. It was an argument about which of them should get to use a famous actor. Goldwyn finally seemed to give in. "Okay," he began to reply, but then made a sudden about-face in the same sentence. "As long as it's understood that I get him."

Goldwyn's inability to get names straight was also legendary. He repeatedly called Joel McCrae, one of his stars, "Joe McRail." When the actor couldn't stand it anymore, he blurted out in a meeting, "It's Joel McCrae, Mr. Goldwyn. Joel McCrae!" To which Goldwyn replied incredulously to the others in the room, "Look! He's telling me how to pronounce his name! And I've got him under contract!"

When Sam Goldwyn wanted to hire director Henry Koster for the film *The Bishop's Wife,* he got Koster's name right, but that was about it. Trying to sweeten the deal, Goldwyn said to Koster, "How would you like to work with Laurette Taylor?"

"I'd love to," replied Koster. "But she's dead."

Goldwyn quickly set the director straight. "Two hours ago," he insisted, "she was sitting right where you are sitting now. And I talked to her!"

When Koster told him he must be mistaken, Goldwyn brought in his secretary and demanded that she settle the matter. "What was that lady's name who was sitting here two hours ago?" he barked. "The actress."

"Loretta Young," replied the secretary.

"See!" Goldwyn told Koster triumphantly. "What did I tell you? She's not dead!"

Although Goldwyn could remember in great detail every time he was crossed in a business deal, he could easily forget what he had been doing a few minutes before.

He once called Darryl Zanuck of Twentieth Century Fox to borrow a Fox movie star for a Goldwyn film — a common arrangement in Hollywood back then. When Zanuck's secretary told Goldwyn that her boss was in a meeting, Goldwyn insisted that she get him immediately. It was urgent, he said.

A few minutes later, when Zanuck got on the phone, Goldwyn was ready. "Yes, Darryl?" he asked politely. "What can I do for you today?"

BENNY GOODMAN

(1909–1986)

They called him the King of Swing, but he was much more than that. At a time when the South was segregated, Benny Goodman was one of the first white bandleaders to put together a racially integrated group. He was also, in 1938, the first jazz musician to perform at Carnegie Hall, helping finally to "legitimize" jazz, as one critic put it.

On the other hand, Goodman was widely considered the most absentminded bandleader of his or any other generation. According to singer Peggy Lee, she and Goodman once jumped into a cab outside the RCA building. While the driver waited for an address,

Goodman sat quietly in the back for several minutes, deep in thought.

Finally the driver spoke up. "Well, buddy?" he demanded. Goodman looked up with a start, took out his wallet, and before the cab had moved an inch, asked how much he owed for the fare.

Another time one of his musicians was fed up with what he believed was Goodman's open disapproval of his performance. First, the bandleader had taken away his solo and given it to someone else, said the musician. And if that weren't bad enough, Goodman kept staring at him with a frown whenever the sideman was playing.

One night after the final set, the musician had had enough. He burst into Goodman's dressing room and shouted, "That's it, Benny! I can't take this anymore! I'm quitting!" Then he slammed the door on his way out.

A puzzled Goodman looked at his manager. "Who was that?" he asked.

Like any great Senior Moments Hall of Famer, Goodman also had trouble with names. He once phoned George Simon, the editor of a jazz magazine, and admitted to him, "Whenever I call your house, I'm always embarrassed if your wife answers because I just can't remember her name."

Goodman then plaintively asked his good friend George for help. "What *is* her name, Bob?"

GEORGE HARVEST

(1716–1780)

In our humble but expert opinion, the archetypal absentminded minister can give the archetypal absentminded professor a run for his or her money on any given day.

Consider George Harvest, the minister of St. Nicholas church (pictured above) in the village of Thames-Ditton in Surrey, England. Harvest was so absentminded that he continually lost track of the time. Not just the time of day, mind you, but the day itself.

On one particular Sunday, which he must have thought was Saturday, the minister walked down to his church with a gun in hand to find out just what all those suspicious people who were sitting inside it were really up to.

Harvest was prone to serious memory lapses long before he reached middle age. As a young man, he became engaged to the bishop of London's daughter. It would have been a fine match for the clergyman if only he had not gone fishing on his wedding day and arrived too late for the ceremony.

The lady was incensed and departed forthwith. And so, instead of landing a prestigious position in London, Harvest remained in the village of Thames-Ditton for the rest of his life.

Incredibly, that was not the only time he forgot to show up for his own wedding at the duly appointed hour. It was merely the first time. He did it again some years later when, delighted by some fine weather, he joined a few friends for lunch. When he suddenly remembered that another important piece of business had been planned for that day, he could not, for the life of him, recall what it was.

His second fiancée turned out to be just as understanding as his first and never spoke to him again.

Reverend Harvest's memory was a perfect sieve through which anything could fall. He was known to write a letter to one person, address it to another, and then adding to the confusion, forget to sign it so the recipient had no idea who had sent it.

In the company of his friends, Harvest's memory was no better. He would forget to pass a bottle of wine at dinner and absentmindedly refill his glass again and again instead. By the end of the meal, he would be quite intoxicated while the rest of his companions remained unhappily sober.

At least no damage was done, unlike the time he was conversing with a small group of acquaintances when a fly began to buzz around the room. Much to Harvest's annoyance, although he kept swatting at the insect, he also kept missing. When it finally settled upon the bonnet of one of the ladies, Harvest saw his chance. He slapped his hand down upon her head without thinking, killing the fly, but also rendering her unconscious.

Even leaving a house could turn out to be a difficult task for Harvest. After dining at a friend's house one evening, he politely bid his host farewell, but instead of going out the front door, he walked up three sets of stairs, all the way to the garret.

Confused, he stomped about in the dark, trying to find his way out. When a maid who was working on the floor below took up a lamp to see who was making such a racket, she found the good reverend. He confessed that he must have taken a wrong turn and begged her to point him in the direction of the street.

This was not the only problem Harvest experienced in other people's homes. He was often discovered sleeping in the wrong one.

His memory lapses also extended to more familiar surroundings. He once absentmindedly locked a friend and his new wife in one of his upstairs bedrooms after showing them where they could sleep. Meaning to come right back, he put the key in his pocket and then forgot about his friends. He went about his business and only realized his mistake when he returned home at night, astonished to find the couple still in the locked room upstairs.

As every senior moment sufferer knows, familiarity can breed absentmindedness as well as contempt, but Harvest seems to have taken this to extremes. After washing up, he would often wipe his hands on his bed sheets and go to sleep with his boots on. He seldom had a clean shirt, and when he did, he either forgot to shave or wore two stockings that didn't match.

Nor did his senior moments stop at the threshold. When a beggar on the street doffed his cap in hope of receiving a coin, Harvest, lost in his thoughts, made the vagrant a low bow in return and declared that he was the man's most obedient and humble servant.

Perhaps the good reverend was on his way to the theater, where senior moments were often known to strike. Consider the time he attended a play in London and sat in a box above the stage. Knowing that he would be staying overnight in the city, he decided to keep his nightcap in his pocket. Unfortunately (but not surprisingly) the nightcap slipped out and fell down to the seats below. It was then tossed from person to person, each one assuming it belonged to the next man or woman in the row.

When Harvest realized what was happening, he demanded that it be returned to him forthwith. Unfortunately he had forgotten that the play was still going on. His outburst disrupted the performance, much to everyone's dismay. But at least he got his nightcap back.

Harvest's reveries and distractions were so frequent that whenever he travelled, he was forced to borrow a horse, having lost his own through inattention. This continued for quite some time until his friends would no longer oblige him because he "misplaced" their horses, too.

How, you might ask, does one manage to misplace a horse? It seems that Harvest liked to dismount near his destination and walk the rest of the way. Putting the reins under one arm, he would often fail to notice that the horse had shaken off its bridle and wandered away, even as Harvest continued to hold on to the reins with no animal attached.

Harvest was never the most alert traveler, to say the least. When he traveled on foot, he insisted on walking down the middle of the road. Unable to pay attention to anything around him, he was nearly run over and killed a number of times.

Sometimes on fishing trips, he would buy snacks to sustain him. He would put them in his waistcoat pocket along with his bait worms and some tobacco for his pipe, and then forget all about them, sometimes for days, until he stank so badly his presence was insufferable.

However, it should be added that Reverend Harvest was known for more than his absentmindedness. He was frequently praised for the high quality of his sermons — although this did not mean he was free of senior moments in the pulpit.

He once brought to church three separate sermons, intending to pick one to preach, but somehow mixed up the sheets of paper and found himself holding a single, long, extremely muddled sermon.

Confused but unwilling to disappoint his flock, he began to read it anyway. But after the first page, he lost his train of thought. The second page was out of order and did not follow the logic of the first, and so he was unable to recite anything from memory. And yet he persisted, even though no one, including himself, could make sense of it.

When he finally looked up, all the pews were empty, his parishioners having fled long before the end.

JAMES HERRIOT

(1916–1995)

Who better than a writer to write amusingly about his own senior moments? James Herriot, the pen name of James Alfred Wight, an English veterinarian, authored a series of charming, semi-autobiographical best sellers beginning in 1972 with *All Creatures Great and Small.*

Interestingly, "Siegfried Farnon," the books' thinly veiled portrait of Herriot's partner, Donald Sinclair, is presented as quite absentminded. But it was Herriot himself who later admitted that his own forgetfulness was "constant and longstanding."

There were the usual senior moments: forgetting where he was going while driving to an appointment, taking a country walk and then forgetting to put his dog in the car before he drove off, brushing his teeth with shaving cream, and putting the wrong letters in the wrong envelopes with all the attendant embarrassment.

But then there were the incidents that merit special honors.

In the first, as Herriot was passing the local grocery store, the manager, Mr. Craythorne, was standing in the doorway. Herriot had known him for years. The shop was called Mead's.

Mr. Craythorne in front of Mead's.

Mead's with Mr. Craythorne in front.

Got it?

"Now then, Mr. Herriot," said Craythorne when the veterinarian, whose mind was elsewhere, slowly walked past him.

Herriot had only to say "good morning" and leave it at that. Instead, he made the obvious mistake of trying to use Craythorne's name in his greeting — a name that escaped him entirely.

Desperately trying to remember it, Herriot's eyes fixed upon the large sign above the grocery, which read MEAD.

He was delighted. This was one senior moment, at least, that would not get the better of him.

"Good morning, Mead!" he cried with a broad smile.

Quickly realizing that his greeting, which only included the manager's last name, might be construed as impolite, not to mention a trifle arrogant, Herriot turned back to Craythorne and said, "Good morning, *Mister* Mead."

It was only when the veterinarian turned the corner that he realized his mistake but was too embarrassed to go back.

Making the whole thing even more humiliating was the fact that it wasn't a good morning at all, but a good late afternoon.

And yet for every senior moment that the chronically absentminded soul must suffer through, there is always another bout of forgetfulness that proves to be worse.

The following had its genesis in a simple request. Herriot's wife asked him to take the sitting-room clock in for repair. So he dutifully drove into their small town, parked, and entered the repair shop with the clock under his arm.

There was one slight problem. He had entered the wrong shop.

Now an ordinary person would notice his mistake immediately. But a Titan of Forgetfulness is no mere mortal, even if the store in question is the butcher's shop, which no one could ever mistake for a repair shop.

Moreover, Herriot had been a loyal customer of the butcher's for years.

The proprietor smiled as Herriot gazed into space with the clock cradled in his arm. He waited for Herriot's order, cleaver in hand.

Seconds passed before the veterinarian finally realized where he was.

An ordinary person (hmm, there's that word "ordinary" again) would have smiled back and ordered a cut of meat or a pound of sausages. But that would presuppose the person's connection with reality had been firmly re-established.

Instead, Herriot nodded, and without saying a single word, turned around and left, leaving the bewildered butcher in his wake.

JEAN DE LA FONTAINE

(1621–1695)

La Fontaine, one of the most widely read poets in 17th century France, is still known today for his satiric *Fables*, featuring animals who reflect the less seemly aspects of human behavior. The fox is devious, the eagle arrogant, the cat deceitful, and so on. But aficionados of senior moments also know the poet for his fabled fits of forgetfulness.

After all, it was La Fontaine who once called at the house of a friend whom he had not seen lately, only to be told that the friend had died six months earlier.

"True! True!" he exclaimed when his memory was jogged. "I went to his funeral!"

Even something as important as a fight to the death could slip his mind. Shortly after challenging a suspected admirer of his wife to a duel, La Fontaine implored the man to pay a visit to his home and break bread with him.

When Louis XIV, one of La Fontaine's greatest admirers, invited him to Versailles to present a copy of *Fables* in person — a signal honor — the poet forgot to bring the book with him.

He was warmly received by the court regardless, and showered with gifts, including a purse full of gold from the king himself. When La Fontaine left the palace, he promptly lost it.

At a time when no gentleman would dream of going out in public in anything less than the perfect attire arranged just so for maximum effect, La Fontaine astonished his friends by spending an entire day walking about Paris with his stockings inside out. Trés gauche.

But perhaps his most telling (and dramatic) senior moment occurred when he attended a social gathering while distracted beyond measure, and walked past by his own son without a second glance.

Others have been known to do the same thing. (See Gerald Ford, for example.) However, La Fontaine topped them all. When told by friends what he had just done, he replied absentmindedly, "Ah, yes, I thought I had seen him somewhere."

WALTER SAVAGE LANDOR

(1775–1864)

The English writer and poet W. S. Landor fought with nearly everyone he met at one time or another, including his wife, his relatives, university functionaries, lords, bishops, Italian dukes, politicians, publishers, and, of course, lawyers — especially lawyers. In his great novel, *Bleak House,* Charles Dickens went so far as to put a thinly disguised version of Landor at the center of an absurd and endless legal dispute.

Although the poet never forgot a slight — or one of his poems —he could forget just about anything else.

Eliza Lynn Linton, a writer herself and once Landor's protégé, could not hide her impatience at her mentor's absentmindedness, even years after his death. He was always losing and overlooking things, she wrote, but it was his reaction to his forgetfulness that most irked her.

"He used to stick a letter into a book; then, when he wanted to answer it, it was gone — and someone had taken it — the only letter he wanted to answer — that he would rather have forfeited a thousand pounds than have lost, and so on. Or he used to push up his spectacles over his forehead and then declare they were lost, 'lost forever.'"

At such times, Landor would stomp around the room, knocking into everything that was in his way, declaring that he was the most unfortunate man in the world, or the greatest fool, or the most persecuted.

"When I would persuade him to sit down and let me look for the lost item," wrote Linton, "he would sigh in deep despair and say there was no use in taking any more trouble about it; it was gone forever."

When Linton found the item, as she invariably did, he would say "thank you" quickly and quietly as if he had not been raving like a lunatic a few moments before.

Some people simply forget, but Landor's forgetfulness was of a higher order. For example, whenever he was invited to spend a weekend at the home of friends, he would fail to remember to bring along the key to his luggage.

One weekend, determined to bring the key with him at last, he carefully put it in his pocket after locking his valise.

Before leaving his house, he patted his pocket and felt the key inside.

During the coach ride, he put his hand in his pocket every few minutes to make sure the key was still there.

Finally, upon arriving at his friend's house, he was overjoyed to find the key had not "escaped" from his pocket. He even showed it to his friend. "You see!" he cried. "I have it with me! I have it with me! I didn't forget it this time!"

But then he suddenly thought of something else and his face fell.

"Oh my God," he moaned, "I forgot the valise!"

A. E. MATTHEWS

(1869–1960)

Alfred Edward Matthews, a consummate character actor who appeared in dozens of films and plays, was prized for his versatility, longevity, and eventually his forgetfulness.

One of Matthews' last performances was in the play, *The Manor of Northstead*. During rehearsals in London, it became clear that Matthews was having trouble remembering his lines.

The director was alarmed, but not Matthews, who sought to reassure him. "I know you think I'm not going to know my lines, but I promise that even if we had to open next Monday, I would be all right."

If Matthews thought he was allaying the director's fears, he was sadly mistaken. "But Matty," the director said anxiously, "we *do* open on Monday!"

In that same year, he suffered another classic senior moment that involved another play. It demonstrated Matthews' extraordinary versatility not only as an actor, but also as a man coping courageously with lapses of memory.

Everything was going smoothly until there was a scene with a telephone call, a call that was crucial to the plot.

It was Matthews who was supposed to answer the phone. When it rang on cue, he crossed the stage and picked up the receiver. And stood there. For what seemed like an eternity.

For the life of him he could not recall his part of the conversation.

In desperation, he turned to the only other actor on stage, held out the phone to him, and blurted out, "It's for you."

His last hurrah came when he was nearly ninety years old. He was attending a celebration of 50 years of filmmaking at Pinewood Studios, located just outside London.

During the luncheon, Sir Leonard Brockington, the first chairman of the Canadian Broadcasting Corporation, delivered a long, rambling speech during which Matthews' mind began to wander. After 25 minutes Brockton paused, prompting several guests to applaud in relief, believing that the speech had finally ended.

But when Brocton started up again, Matthews' brain did not. Unaware that his muttering could be heard throughout the room, he groused, "My God, doesn't he know I haven't got long to live?"

MARILYN MONROE

(1926–1962)

So young and yet so forgetful, proving once again that senior moments are not just for seniors.

For all her genuine personal problems, Marilyn Monroe was hardly alone in Hollywood's over-crowded Celebrity Hell. And yet she was still able to set a new standard for forgetfulness among film stars — a standard that has never been equaled.

First of all, Monroe could never remember when she was supposed to arrive for work. During the production of *The Seven Year Itch*, she showed up at eleven o'clock for an eight-thirty start. Her excuse? Unable to find the studio, she got lost — even though she had been under contract there for six years.

Second, she excelled at forgetting lines. One scene in *Some Like It Hot* required 83 takes. She simply could not remember the line, "It's me...Sugar."

Afterwards, director Billy Wilder tried to reassure Monroe, telling her not to worry about it. But this only served to confuse her further. "Worry about what?" she asked.

Some Like It Hot was not only one of the best Hollywood comedies ever made, but also a perfect showcase for Monroe's formidable absentmindedness. Another scene called for her to enter a room, walk over to a dresser, open various drawers looking for a bottle of bourbon, and then ask her co-stars, Tony Curtis and Jack Lemmon, for a drink. But somehow that single line eluded her. Finally, on the 53rd take, Wilder had a member of the crew write the line on different pieces of paper and put one in each drawer so that all she had to do was look down and read it.

It should have been a foolproof plan, except for one unforeseen problem. She walked over to the wrong piece of furniture.

On the set of her last movie, *Something's Got to Give*, which Monroe never finished, she was hopelessly late to rehearsals and shoots. Billy Wilder, again the director, needed her for a scene one morning, but was unable to find her. "It used to be you'd call her at nine AM and she'd show up at noon," he complained. "Now you call her in May and she shows up in October."

On the other hand, Monroe's extraordinary chemistry was indisputable. "My Aunt Minnie would be punctual and never hold up production," Wilder reflected. "But who would pay to see my Aunt Minnie?"

MICHEL DE MONTAIGNE

(1533–1592)

Michel de Montaigne didn't merely have memory lapses. He spun them into philosophical gold. Let him stand as an inspiration to us all!

Born into a rich family near Bordeaux, Montaigne had the means and inclination to make himself the subject of a series of famous essays. Centuries later the autobiographical essay may be commonplace, but Montaigne was the first to establish it as a literary genre. (It could be argued that he wrote with more honesty, humor, and brilliance than anyone since.)

Montaigne was a master of mixing casual anecdotes about his life with deep reflections on human nature, always striving for utter frankness. Some of his shortcomings pained him, but others he accepted calmly, including his chronic forgetfulness.

He admitted cheerfully that he forgot most of the things he read. The more significant a fact, the more likely it would slip through his memory. "So greatly do I excel in forgetfulness," he confessed, "that even my writings…are forgotten with the rest."

If Montaigne thought of something to look up in his library, he was forced to "confide his need to someone else" lest he forget it while walking across the courtyard to get there.

He routinely forgot the names of his servants, even if they had been with him for years, and was forced to call them by their function "If I should have a long life, I believe I should forget my own name," he said.

It took him three hours to learn two verses of poetry — this in an era when one's ability to quote at length from memory was an essential skill of public life. And Montaigne's life was as public as any person's. He served as the mayor of Bordeaux and was a confidant of the king. Yet his mind often went blank when he tried to speak extemporaneously before an audience of any significant size. "If I grow so bold as to break my thread [of thought] ever so little, I never fail to lose it altogether," he explained.

However, after much reflection he concluded that a poor memory was not a liability but an asset.

It kept his speeches and anecdotes short and to the point, he decided, simply because he could not remember long ones.

It improved his reasoning because he had to get to the heart of the matter before his mind wandered.

It forced him to jettison unimportant information out of necessity.

"Forget much of what you learn," Montaigne counseled.

Reassuring advice for all of us who, in just the last few moments since we read it, have already begun to forget it.

SIR ISAAC NEWTON

(1642–1727)

Sir Isaac Newton, "Scientific Genius," needs no introduction, but Sir Isaac Newton, "Titan of Forgetfulness," probably does.

Dr. William Stukeley, Sir Isaac's friend and a fellow member of the Royal Society, wrote extensively about Newton's "extreme absence of mind" in his book, *Memoirs of Sir Isaac Newton's Life.*

"He dressed slovenly, was rather languid, and was often so absorbed in his own thoughts as to be anything but a lively companion," Stukeley recounted. "On the few occasions when he sacrificed his time to entertain his friends, if he left them to get more wine, or for any similar reason, he would as often as not be found, after the lapse of some time, working out a problem, oblivious alike of his expectant guests and of his errand."

When Newton was the Lucasian Professor of Mathematics at Cambridge University, he rarely visited the faculty dining hall. But if he did, said Stukeley, "He would go very carelessly, with shoes down at heels, stockings untied, and his head scarcely combed."

At other times, Sir Isaac would set out for the dining hall but never arrive. "He would turn to the left hand and go out into the street, then making a stop when he found he had made a mistake, would hastily turn back, and then, instead of going to the hall, he would return to his chamber again."

Newton was well known for begrudging the short time he "wasted" eating and sleeping — if he remembered to eat and sleep at all. On one occasion, Stukeley called on Newton only to find out that the mathematician was working in his study with strict orders not to be disturbed. So Stukeley waited and waited.

Stukeley assumed, reasonably enough, that after a servant brought a roast chicken for Newton's dinner and left it on a table, Sir Isaac would arrive soon after. But as the clock ticked away, impatience and hunger got the better of Stukeley. Without thinking (sharing that peculiarity with Sir Isaac, perhaps), Stukeley sat down at the table and began to eat the chicken.

When Newton finally left his study and greeted his friend, he sat down at the table for his long-delayed meal. As an embarrassed Stukeley waited for his reaction, Newton gazed down at the plate of chicken bones and remarked that since the chicken had been eaten, he must have eaten himself and then forgotten all about it.

In another celebrated bout of absentmindedness, Newton used his fiancée's finger to tamp down the tobacco in his pipe. (There is no record of her reaction, but suffice it to say he never married.)

His most public senior moment came when he served as Cambridge University's representative to Parliament in 1689. When he rose to speak before the House of Commons, there was an expectant silence as his fellow parliamentarians awaited the great man's maiden speech. But alas, Newton's mind had wandered. After a long pause, he commented distractedly that a window had been left open and was causing a draft. He asked that it be closed immediately and promptly sat down. And that was that. He never addressed Parliament again.

RICHARD NIXON

(1913–1994)

Richard Nixon was so demonized over the years that his numerous senior moments now serve to humanize him.

First on the list was his inability to remember names. For example, he could never quite master the name of his assistant attorney general, William Rehnquist. A month after they were introduced, Nixon was still calling him "Renchburg." Even a few weeks before Nixon nominated Rehnquist to the Supreme Court, he was referring to him as "Bill Rensler."

Once, while the President was shaking hands at an airport, a little girl shouted, "How is Smokey the Bear?"'

(A bruin stand-in for the famous fire-fighting bear was residing at the Washington National Zoo at the time.)

Unable to make out her words, Nixon smiled and turned away, but the girl kept waving furiously and repeating her question. Nixon finally turned to an aide, who whispered in his ear, "Smokey the Bear, Washington National Zoo." Unable to retain the information for even a few seconds without garbling it, Nixon walked over to the girl, shook her hand, and said, "How do you do, Miss Bear?"

But Nixon's verbal senior moments went far beyond names. A truck hit the policeman leading Nixon's presidential motorcade through St. Petersburg, Florida, in 1970. When Nixon hurried to the scene to offer his sympathies to the injured officer, the policeman apologized for holding up the motorcade.

An awkward silence ensued as Nixon searched his mind for something else to say to the man — hopefully, something appropriate. Surely it was in there somewhere, but where?

Finally Nixon blurted out, "So, do you like the work?"

And then there was the time he visited Paris to attend the 1974 funeral of French president, Georges Pompidou. At the airport, Nixon forgot his prepared remarks and declared instead, "This is a great day for France!"

Even reporters who covered him were sometimes taken aback by the President's senior moments. Veteran CBS journalist Bob Schieffer, for one, will always remember the time he asked Nixon an innocent question at the White House.

"There had been this story going around that the president was bringing in some new advisors," Schieffer recalled. "But we didn't know if they were going to hire [outside] people... So when it came to my turn, I shook hands with the President and said, 'Sir, about these advisors, will these be in-house advisors?' And he said, 'No, they will be out-house advisors.'"

RICHARD PORSON

(1759–1808)

It's comforting to know that even someone with an unusually keen memory can be prone to serious senior moments, too, a duality greatly prized here at the Senior Moments Hall of Fame.

Consider the classics scholar Richard Porson, who held the prestigious Regius Greek Professorship at Cambridge University from 1792 until his death in 1808. Porson was once asked the meaning of a certain word in Thucydides' *History of the Peloponnesian War.* Instead of replying with a mere definition, he repeated the entire passage in which the word was used.

Not once did Porson forget something he had read. As a student at Eton, his memory was the stuff of legend. One day he was called upon in class to recite in Latin some verses from Horace, the great Roman poet. But having forgotten to bring his own classics book, he gratefully accepted one that was suddenly thrust into his hands by a mischievous classmate sitting next to him.

Porson did not skip a beat. He recited the excerpt with perfect accuracy. But his eagle-eyed teacher became suspicious when he noticed that Porson wasn't looking at the upper part of the page on which the lesson was printed, but the lower part. A small thing perhaps, but students had been punished for less.

Snatching the book from Porson's hand to examine it closely, the lecturer discovered it was an English translation of Ovid's *Metamorphoses*, not Horace. Everything that Porson had read aloud was from memory.

On the other hand, when it came to mundane tasks that most people would find easy to remember, Porson's absentmindedness often got the better of him.

He never remembered to answer letters and sometimes remained incommunicado for days or weeks. Completely absorbed in the work of translation, he forgot to tell his friends and colleagues where he would be, what he would be doing, or when he would reappear, so they often feared the worst.

When asked to dinner by a friend, he once replied absentmindedly, "Thank you, no, I dined yesterday."

When he did dine with friends, he often paid no attention to what he was drinking. One evening at the house of his friend Hoppner, the famous portrait painter, Porson was told by his host that, alas, he could offer him no wine because Mrs. Hoppner, who was out at the time, had taken the wine cellar keys with her.

Porson was convinced that there must be a spare bottle lying around somewhere in the house, and was triumphant when he found one in a drawer. Without thinking (or sniffing, or tasting), he promptly drained what he assumed were spirits of some kind, and then distractedly returned to the table to finish his dinner.

When Mrs. Hoppner returned and heard what had happened, she cried out, "Drunk it? Good God! It was for the lamp!"

Porson's memory was also less than stellar when it came to his clothing. He took so little trouble over his appearance as to shock some of his colleagues. One contemporary account describes him "with a large patch of coarse brown paper on his nose" (how it got there was a mystery) and "his rusty black coat hung with cobwebs."

He was sometimes turned away by his friends' servants, who assumed he was a beggar. And restaurants where he was expected often denied him entrance.

But perhaps the crowning achievement in his life of senior moments came when he got married. As a 19th century biographer related, "One night he was smoking his pipe with George Gordon at the Cider Cellar when he suddenly said, 'Friend George, do you not think the Widow Lunan an agreeable sort of personage?' Gordon said something in the affirmative. 'In that case, ' continued Porson, 'you must meet me tomorrow morning at St. Martin's-in-the Fields at eight o'clock.'"

Porson paid the bill without another word and went home straightaway.

Gordon, who was taken aback by this unexpected news, followed Porson's instructions to the letter. He arrived at the church at the appointed hour and found Porson, Mrs. Lunan, a friend of hers, and a parson. But immediately after the ceremony, Porson returned to his bachelor ways. He absentmindedly ambled off in a different direction from his new wife and then spent the rest of the day and night eating, drinking, and conversing with Gordon.

There is no record of Mrs. Porson's reaction when her husband finally remembered that he might possibly be expected home to attend to his new wife.

On the other hand, at least Porson showed up for the marriage ceremony, unlike poor, befuddled Reverend Harvest.

AndrÉ PREVIN

(1929–)

The pianist, composer, and conductor André Previn got an early start on his life of senior moments. As a teenager, he had a job playing the piano at a movie theater specializing in silent films. He was playing the appropriate music for a Roaring Twenties feature called *Flaming Youth* one afternoon when he became so absorbed with the score that he forgot to look up at the screen, which every new accompanist had been warned about repeatedly. As a result, he did not notice that the Jazz Age melodrama had ended and the main attraction, D. W. Griffith's biblical epic, *Intolerance,* had begun.

So there he was, enthusiastically pounding out an up-tempo Charleston during a scene depicting the Last Supper.

His job lasted a few moments more — the time it took for the horrified theater manager to storm down the aisle and fire him.

As Previn's career soared, his senior moments remained steady. One evening, after a rehearsal with the London Symphony Orchestra, he retired to a hotel bar for a well-deserved drink with the soloist, a young pianist.

While waiting for her, Previn spied an American composer whose work he admired. Previn waved him over and insisted on buying him a drink.

The composer was full of praise. "I heard your orchestra a few nights ago. It sounded absolutely marvelous," he said, then added with a smile, "It was the night when Beethoven's Sixth was played in the second half."

"Oh God," Previn replied with dismay, "that was the night [the great Italian pianist Maurizio] Pollini was supposed to play the Fourth Piano Concerto in the second half, but he cancelled. And we were stuck with one of those last-minute substitutions, a really appalling third-rate pianist. I'm really sorry you had to suffer through that."

Had Previn searched his memory, he might have remembered one all-important fact about the composer who sat before him. Even a quick glance at the young man's face might have been sufficient. But once again, Previn forgot to look up.

"That's all right, I didn't mind," the composer said coldly. "That pianist was my wife."

And then there was the time Previn and his wife decided to adopt a Vietnamese orphan. A certain Miss Taylor, who had run an orphanage in Saigon, was assigned to assess the Previns' suitability during the course of a weekend, staying at their apartment Friday and Saturday night to observe them especially closely.

At breakfast Saturday morning, Miss Taylor asked if she might have a bowl of cereal.

"Of course," said Previn.

Anxious that the visit go smoothly, he distractedly reached for the large jar of health-food cereal that his two small sons were fond of. He then poured a generous serving into her bowl and passed her the milk.

As Miss Taylor ate in silence, Previn explained all the virtues of the cereal, especially its nutritional value.

"To be quite honest, I'm not crazy about it," she said when she finished.

It was then that Previn took a closer look at the jar and realized he had just served the woman who would decide his suitability as a parent a heaping bowl of hamster food.

BARONESS VICTORIA
SACKVILLE-WEST

(1862–1936)

These days the gloriously eccentric Lady Victoria Sackville-West is chiefly remembered (if at all) for giving birth to author Vita Sackville-West, the lover of Virginia Woolf. But the baroness was an important figure in her own right, not to mention a woman whose senior moments were a wonder.

She once left a bank check for £10,000 in the back of a taxi. The check was made out to "Bearer," so anyone lucky enough to find it could cash it without identification, which probably explains why the money was never recovered.

It was an impressive loss. £10,000 in the 1920's would be worth about £850,000 today, or $1.4 million. But happily for her, the Baroness had the gift of forgetting her forgetfulness, and quickly moved on to her next lapse of memory.

Perhaps the best indicator of Sackville-West's absent-mindedness was an incident involving a charity she established to help fund, well, herself, actually.

She called it the Million Penny Fund and claimed it was meant to eliminate Britain's National Debt, when it was really intended to help her fund her vast estate. (Losing a £10,000 check couldn't have helped her financial situation all that much.)

This was not an example of forgetfulness, however, but her impressive ability to lie with a straight face. No, the senior moment came later.

After the Baroness had scoured newspapers and magazines for the birthdays of famous people, she sent them all a letter asking if they would contribute one penny for each year of their lives.

She concluded with a request that only someone experiencing a severe lapse of memory (such as herself) would forget to edit. "And do give me three stamped envelopes," she entreated. "One for my [next] begging letter, one for having the pleasure of thanking you, and one for a fresh victim."

Alas, there is no record of how many victims were willing to victimize someone else, and sent the Baroness the envelopes she had requested.

GEORGE SALMON

(1819–1904)

George Salmon was a triple threat in the senior moments world. He started out as an absent-minded mathematician and ended up as an absentminded professor of divinity and an absentminded college provost.

A visitor was strolling one Sunday morning through the campus of Trinity College in Dublin when he saw coming towards him none other than George Salmon, "a venerable figure with side-whiskers and a formidable reputation for learning."

The visitor politely raised his hat to the great man and received a courteous acknowledgement in turn.

A few moments after the encounter, the visitor began to wonder if had just seen something extraordinary or had simply imagined it. To find out, he ran around the buildings that stood along the opposite side in order to pass Salmon a second time.

Once again, they exchanged a silent, amiable greeting. But this time, the visitor was able to verify his first impression. He had been right, after all. The Provost's pants were on backwards.

As the college's Regius Professor of Divinity, Salmon delivered a sermon each Sunday. But one day he mistakenly brought to church the same sermon he preached the year before.

Unable to think of anything else to do, he pressed on regardless, and read from the text.

Later, he explained his reasoning this way, as only a former mathematician would do:

Surely half the congregation had not been in church the year before, so the sermon would be new to them.

One quarter may have heard the sermon, but those people were just as absentminded as Salmon was, and had no doubt forgotten it.

As for those in the final quarter of the congregation, they would be happy to hear it again since it was really rather good, if he dared say himself.

Perhaps he was thinking about another sermon he forgot he had delivered before, when he was found sitting on a curb one morning, staring blankly at the sky. His senior moment was so prolonged, and his clothing in such a neglected state, that a kind old lady stopped in front of him. Thinking he was a blind beggar, she offered to take his hand and lead him safely across the street.

ALEXANDER SCRIABIN

(1871–1915)

Scriabin, the great Russian composer and pianist, was one of the most innovative and controversial creators of early modern classical music. It was written of him, "No composer had more scorn heaped [upon him] or greater love bestowed...."

Although he influenced such modern masters as Stravinsky and Prokofiev, who were happy to champion him, he disliked the music of both men. And yet in spite of his prickliness and eccentricity, Scriabin remained a favorite composer of contemporary pianists.

But it was his notorious absentmindedness, not his music, which so impressed the curators of the Senior Moments Hall of Fame.

His music publisher, M. P. Belaieff, continually tried to persuade Scriabin to make sure his compositions were accurate before he sent them off. Scriabin often forgot to put in notations for tempo, volume, phrasing, and mood.

Sending letters to the right person at the right place in a timely fashion also gave Scriabin great difficulty. One letter from Belaieff insisted that the composer copy the publisher's instructions and send them back to him, as one might instruct a child. Contrite, Scriabin wrote back, "You ask me to write you where I'm supposed to send my manuscripts. I will say first of all that I'm frightfully ashamed of being so absentminded."

His apology to Belaieff notwithstanding, Scriabin could be testy when other people brought up his lapses in memory. He once received two letters, the first from Rimsky-Korsakov and the second from Anatoly Liadov, the Russian pianist, conductor, and teacher. Both men good-naturedly chided Scriabin for his forgetfulness.

Unamused, the composer dashed off replies to both of them, defending himself at great length.

In due time he received a letter back from Liadov. Inside the envelope was Scriabin's letter to Rimsky-Korsakov, mistakenly addressed to Liadov.

Scriabin was so forgetful that he once arrived at a party wearing a pair of brand new boots, only to leave wearing two old, worn-out boots. He had no idea how it might have happened, or to whom the old boots belonged.

Even more mysteriously, they didn't even match.

Always short of money, Scriabin misplaced so many gloves, umbrellas, shoes, boots, and various articles of clothing that he finally instructed his family to stop him from leaving the house if he was wearing anything new. He insisted they restrict him to second-hand items only.

Clearly, being absentminded doesn't mean you have to be impractical, too.

ADAM SMITH

(1723–1790)

He was the legendary Scottish author of *The Wealth of Nations*, still one of the world's most influential economics treatises nearly 250 years after it was first published. He was also widely praised for his almost photographic memory when it came to facts. And yet he often forgot what he was doing while he was doing it.

Adam Smith's friends, who were legion, were accustomed to the scholar's senior moments, which might strike at any time. Once, while on a tour of a Glasgow tannery, Smith was so preoccupied that he fell into a deep tanning pit from which he had to be rescued.

Even the way he walked was a testament to his absent-mindedness. His head moved from side to side while his body swayed "vermicularly," as one contemporary put it. With each step, he appeared to be on the verge of altering his direction or even going back the way he came. At the same time, his lips moved silently as if in rapt conversation with invisible companions.

Friends loved to talk about the night Smith got out of bed and wandered into his garden while absorbed in some line of reasoning. Had he stayed on his property, he would have been just another deep thinker working out an idea in the middle of the night. But Smith was not like anyone else. He wandered 15 miles in his dressing gown before he suddenly stopped in the middle of the road, confounded as to where he was and how he got there.

Sir Walter Scott, a contemporary, wrote down two anecdotes that cemented Smith's reputation:

In the first, Dr. Smith was about to sign a document in his official capacity as a commissioner of the Scottish Board of Customs when his mind began to wander. Instead of signing his own name, Smith copied the signature of the commissioner who went before him.

In the second anecdote, Smith "put an elderly maiden lady who presided at a tea-table to sore confusion by utterly neglecting her invitation to be seated, [walking] round and round in a circle instead, stopping ever and anon to steal a lump from the sugar basin, which the venerable spinster was constrained to place on her own knee as the only method of securing it from his uneconomical depredations."

A curious characteristic of the senior moment is that it can afflict even those with a razor-sharp intellect, which explains how the world's first great economist could also excel at falling into a deep reverie at the strangest moments in the strangest ways.

For example, one morning Smith was talking to a friend as they approached a guard in front of the Customs House in Edinburgh. The guard presented his pike in salute and began to lead the way to the boardroom where Dr. Smith was expected.

This guard had escorted Smith countless times before, but on this occasion, for some inexplicable reason, Smith followed closely behind him, imitating each and every one of his motions while brandishing his cane as if it were a pike. Until, that is, Smith suddenly snapped out of it. He continued his conversation with his friend exactly where he had left off, with no recollection of what he had done.

WILLIAM A. SPOONER

(1844–1930)

You probably know the good reverend's name from the linguistic term *spoonerism* — a slip of the tongue that transposes letters or syllables of key words in a given phrase. Dr. Spooner himself uttered one of the most famous examples: Instead of "through a glass darkly," he said, "through a dark glassly"

Although most of the spoonerisms attributed to Spooner himself are apocryphal, his reputation for eccentricity and absentmindedness is indisputable. This, after all, was a man who remarked after meeting a woman who was recently widowed, "A shocking business. Her husband died in the South Seas, you know. Eaten by missionaries."

And while others might pour salt on a spill of red wine to avoid staining a tablecloth, he poured red wine on spilled salt.

Dr. William Archibald Spooner spent his entire career at Oxford University. After enrolling as an undergraduate in 1862, he remained at the university for over 60 years, lecturing on ancient history and philosophy and eventually rising to the level of Warden of Oxford's New College.

A highly respected professor and administrator, Spooner was held in great esteem by students, faculty, and staff. But he was better known for his senior moments, much to Spooner's annoyance.

One day, a colleague received a message asking him to come to Spooner's office the following morning on an urgent matter. That is to say, it *had* been an urgent matter when Spooner began the note. But by the time he got to the end, he was adding a postscript, which explained that the matter had since been resolved and there was no need to come, after all.

Another time, Spooner invited a colleague to a special dinner. "Do come and meet our new Fellow, Casson," he urged.

"But Warden," the man answered, "I am Casson."

"Never mind," said Spooner. "Come anyway."

Confusion reigned among his students as well. When Spooner rebuked one hapless young man for a lackluster oral presentation, the student protested that he had not said a word.

Spooner nodded sagely. "Ah, I thought you hadn't," he said.

JAMES JOSEPH SYLVESTER

(1814–1897)

There's something about higher mathematics that must induce absentmindedness. Along with André-Marie Ampère, Isaac Newton, Paul Erdös, and George Salmon, we're proud to include the esteemed English mathematician, James Joseph Sylvester, in the Senior Moments Hall of Fame.

Professor Sylvester, who first taught at John Hopkins University and then at Oxford, made fundamental contributions in number theory, matrix theory, invariant theory, and other theories you have little hope of understanding. But if you did understand them, you might actually remember them, unlike Sylvester.

One of his former students, W. P. Durfee, who became Professor of Mathematics at Hobart and William Smith Colleges, recalled that Sylvester "had one remarkable peculiarity. He seldom remembered theorems, propositions, etc., but always had to deduce them when he wished to use them."

Elaborating, Durfee wrote, "I remember once submitting to Sylvester some investigations that I had been engaged on, and he immediately denied my first statement, saying that such a proposition had never been heard of, let alone proved. To his astonishment, I showed him a paper of his own in which he had proved the proposition."

Another student had the following experience: On the first day of class, Sylvester declared that to begin with, "Three lectures will be delivered on a New Universal Algebra."

The students were hardly surprised when those "three lectures" took up the entire year.

Moreover, when Sylvester taught a course about Eugen Netto's "Substitution Theories," Netto was completely forgotten within two weeks and never mentioned again.

During one lecture, Sylvester stated a particular theorem and then added, "I haven't proved this, but I am as sure as I can be of anything that it must be true." But at the next lecture he was as sure as he could be of anything that the same theorem must be false.

His smartest students may have been the ones who took notes using a pencil with an eraser instead of a pen.

WILLIAM HOWARD TAFT

(1857–1930)

William Howard Taft simply could not remember names, not even the ones of his staunchest supporters. At one rally, he confessed to a big contributor, "My advisers tell me I *ought* to remember you, but bless my soul, I cannot recall you at all!"

Needless to say, the supporter withdrew his support.

It cannot be easy spending a lifetime in politics without having a keen memory for names and faces. But somehow Taft managed to serve as Solicitor General, a Federal Appeals Court judge, Governor General of the Philippines, a high-level government envoy, Secretary of War under Theodore Roosevelt, the 27th President of the

United States, and Chief Justice while being plagued by senior moments throughout.

On the other hand, Taft *was* defeated for a second term as President, so perhaps he did pay a penalty, after all.

Once, as Secretary of War, he was greeting visitors at a White House reception when his military aide, following standard protocol, asked for the names of the people standing in the receiving line so he could present them properly to the Secretary and his wife. One man, however, adamantly refused to comply. He explained to the aide that because he and Taft were old friends, there was no need for an introduction.

As it turned out, there was a need. When the man reached the front of the line and stood expectantly before the Secretary and his wife, Taft looked at him at blankly, and waited for his aide to make the usual introduction. But this time the aide could only shrug.

Taft was then forced to fall back on the absentminded politician's favorite ploy: a big smile, a hearty handshake, and a turn to the wife with a "You remember our dear old friend here, don't you?"

The future president later confided to Mrs. Taft, "My darling, I have not the faintest idea who he is, but I saw he was an intimate friend by the way he stood poised on one foot waiting to be recognized."

As the aide wrote in his memoir, any time Taft called someone "Old Man," "Old Boy," or "Old Friend," he had no idea who that person was.

(You might want to use this ploy yourself if you don't already.)

Repeated contact did not seem to help Taft at all. He saw the same eight reporters nearly every day when he was in Roosevelt's cabinet, but never learned any of their names or the newspapers they worked for.

One of the reporters was Dick Lindsay of the Kansas City *Star*. When the owner of the *Star*, and Lindsay's boss, Colonel W. R. Nelson, met Taft in Washington, he happened to mention Lindsay.

"Lindsay?" asked a puzzled Taft. "Who's he?"

The next day, after an extremely unpleasant conversation with Colonel Nelson, Dick Lindsay confronted Taft.

"Take a good look at me, will you, Mr. Secretary? I want you to remember what I look like, so the next time you talk to my boss, you will be able to describe me. I'm Lindsay of the Kansas City *Star*!"

Taft laughed uproariously. But he never did remember Lindsay's name.

ELLEN TERRY

(1847 – 1928)

Born into a family of actors, Ellen Terry was widely considered Britain's leading Shakespearean actress in the late 19th century. And yet in spite of her fame and the adulation of her admirers, she was refreshingly honest about her failings, which included embarrassing lapses of memory.

She once confessed that while playing the blind princess Iolanthe, she forgot that she was blind, not once, but twice.

The first time occurred when she saw two of her fellow (and quite near-sighted) actors desperately searching the floor for an amulet they had dropped during a critical scene. The prop, central to the story, was supposed to cure her blindness. But in this case her sight was miraculously restored beforehand for just enough time to allow her to stoop down, pick it up, and hand it to them.

The second time, she put out her hand to stop her co-star from stepping on a bunch of flowers that she shouldn't have been able to see in the first place, and then making things worse, shouted, "Look out for my lilies!"

(Although the line was certainly not in the play, she delivered it with great conviction.)

Like many actors, Terry became very nervous on first nights. But this was especially true during a production of *Henry VIII*. As she explained later, she came to the theater and announced, "I'm going to break down tonight. I can tell you the very line — it's in the scene with the two cardinals. I'm going to dry up." (In theatrical jargon, "to dry up" was to go blank and forget one's line.)

"But if you know the line, why dry up?" she was asked.

"I can't tell you why, but I know I shall," she said.

And so she did.

She was willing to try anything to memorize her part. While studying for her role in the 1893 play, *Madame Sans-Gêne*, one of her most famous, she decided to eliminate all possible distractions. So she traveled to an extremely quiet seaside resort and got down to work (when she wasn't distracted by the sea, that is).

She never did learn all her lines.

Prompters were always on call during a Terry performance as extra insurance against an especially bad memory lapse. (Her usual run-of-the-mill memory lapses were finessed by her consummate skill as an actress with a genius for improvisation.)

On one opening night, prompters were placed wherever they could hide out of sight: behind the backdrop scenery painted on fabric, the set's window curtains and doors, at both sides of the stage, behind the black curtains at the back, and even in a prop "fireplace."

The first moment she paused to search her memory for the next word in her speech, she was bombarded by an incomprehensible volley of whispers from every part of the stage. She finally broke character, clapped her hands in exasperation, and cried out, "Will nobody give me the word?"

In her autobiography, Terry tells of an instance when her adherence to theatrical tradition caused an unfortunate chain reaction. It was a superstition among actors never to say the last few words of a play at a rehearsal. As a result, during all rehearsals of *The Rivals* in which she played the role of Julia, she would murmur, "Mum, mum, mum" instead.

Julia's last few words before the curtain fell were supposed to be, "whose thorn offends them when its leaves are dropped," a line which required Terry to lower her voice at the end. That lowering of tone would be the verbal cue to the full company that her speech was finished and the curtain could come down. But after many days of "mum, mum, mum," Terry forgot exactly how her last words were supposed to be delivered, and she ended instead with an upward inflection.

Now this may seem trivial, but in a profession where people are forced to listen to countless repetitions of the same words, the meaning of those words may begin to blur, leaving inflection as the most important cue to the rest of the company.

As Terry wrote of her senior moment, "The prompter was so astounded [by the upward inflection], he thought there was more coming and did not give the [sign] for the curtain to come down. There was a horrid pause while it remained up, and then [hard-of-hearing actor] J.B. Buckstone exclaimed loudly and irritably, 'Eh? Eh? What does this mean? Why the devil don't you bring down the curtain?'" And he went on cursing until it was finally lowered before an astounded audience.

RUBE WADDELL

(1876–1914)

Hall of Fame pitcher Rube Waddell led the Major Leagues in strikeouts for six straight years during the so-called "dead-ball era." This was a time when most hitters just tried to make contact with the ball, instead of swinging for the fences and just flying out. (It took a change in the manufacture of the balls to make them livelier and thus remedy the problem.)

Waddell was also one of baseball's first celebrities. According to his biographer, he was the first player to have teams of newspaper reporters following him, and the first to have a mass following of idol-worshiping kids yelling out his nickname as if he was their buddy. But that's not why we pay tribute to him here. It was his extraordinary absentmindedness that made him a true Titan of Forgetfulness.

Once during the late innings of a game, Waddell was in the batter's box, waiting for a pitch to hit. Suddenly the catcher squatting behind him rifled a throw to second base, trying to pick off Waddell's teammate, who had strayed from the base. The throw was wild, however, and the ball sailed into centerfield.

It now looked as if Waddell's teammate would be able to score all the way from second because of the error, and Waddell's team, the Philadelphia Athletics, would finally take the lead. But when the center fielder picked up the ball and threw it back to the catcher, trying to beat the runner to the plate, Waddell, without thinking, took a mighty swing at the ball as if it were a pitch and hit it into the seats.

In other circumstances, it would have been a home run, but not in this case. According to the rules, a batter (that would be Waddell) must step aside and keep out of the way as the play unfolds. The last thing Waddell should have done was swing at the ball. Instead of scoring a run, the Athletics watched in horror as the umpire called the runner out for "interference" — Waddell's interference, that is — thus ending the inning.

When the stunned Athletics manager asked Waddell why in the world he did it (using much more vivid language), the pitcher replied simply that it sure looked like a great pitch to hit to him.

To say that Rube Waddell was often distracted would be a gross understatement. He was almost always distracted. On the days he pitched, the fans of the opposing team would hold up shiny objects and even puppies in an attempt to put him into a trance.

At other times, when Waddell was not pitching, he might wander off, only to be found later selling peanuts or hotdogs up in the stands, or playing marbles with kids under the stands, or wrestling bears or alligators at the local zoo, or working alongside local firemen battling fires.

He might be found anywhere, that is, except sitting next to his teammates.

NORBERT WIENER

(1894–1964)

Yes, it's true! We have yet another mathematician who deserves a place of honor in the Senior Moments Hall of Fame: Norbert Wiener of the Massachusetts Institute of Technology.

One of Wiener's contemporaries, K. W. Deutsch, wrote that he must have met in Cambridge, the home of MIT and Harvard, at least 20 people who had won Nobel Prizes or would win them in later years, "But it seemed to me that Norbert was literally more gifted than anyone else."

And, it should go without saying, more absent-minded.

Here's how Chinese physicist C.K. Jen described a class that Wiener taught at MIT:

"Professor Wiener would pay very little attention to his class and would seldom announce the subject of his lecture. He would face the blackboard, standing very close to it because he was extremely near-sighted. Although I usually sat in the front row, I had difficulty seeing what he wrote. Most of the other students could not see anything at all.

"It was most amusing to the class to hear Professor Wiener saying to himself, 'This is very wrong, definitely.' He would quickly erase all he had written down. He would then start all over again, and sometimes murmur to himself, 'This looks all right, so far.'"

Minutes later, Wiener would say, "This cannot be right, either," and he would rub it out once more. This on-again off-again process would continue until the bell signaled the end of the hour, at which point Wiener would leave the room without looking back at his students.

The office of Phyllis Block, a graduate school administrator in MIT's Department of Mathematics, was just a couple of doors down from Wiener's, and he often stopped by to talk. When she moved to another office a few years later, however, he came in to introduce himself, as if for the first time. "He didn't realize I was the same person he had frequently visited," she recalled. "I was in a new office, so he thought I was someone else."

Cars loom large in the Wiener legend. Once, when he went to a conference, he left his car in a large campus parking lot. When the conference was over, he went straight to the lot, but like many of us, forgot where he parked his car. However, *unlike* almost all of us, he also forgot what was his car looked like. He had to wait until all the other cars in the lot were driven away before he could take the one that was left.

This was clearly a man who did not expect his memory to kick in soon. He knew better than that.

Another time, he drove 150 miles to Yale University for a symposium, but when it was over, he forgot he had come by car and returned home to Cambridge by bus. The next morning, when he went out to his garage to get his car, he realized it was missing. Still in the grips of his senior moment — which lasted most of his life, one might say — Wiener contacted the local police to report that while he was away, someone had stolen it.

But perhaps the most famous Wiener anecdote concerns his family's move from Cambridge to the nearby suburb of Newton. Wiener's wife assumed (correctly, of course) that her notoriously absentminded husband would never remember where the new house was or even that they had moved. So she wrote down the address on a piece of paper and handed it to Wiener just before the moving truck arrived.

Off he went to work as usual, until a few hours later an idea suddenly occurred to him. He searched his pockets for something to write on and found the scrap of paper, which he didn't recognize as the note with his new address.

He first scribbled down a few notes, but then, after he had thought about the idea for a bit longer, decided it was worthless and threw the piece of paper away — and with it, the address.

With no note to remind him he was supposed to go to the new house in Newton, Wiener returned to Cambridge. It was there that he found his daughter waiting for him in front of their former, and now empty house.

"Hi, Daddy," she greeted him. "Mommy thought you would forget."

SARAH WINCHESTER

(1839–1922)

An ordinary senior moment is forgetting where you put your keys in a given room. An extraordinary senior moment is forgetting where you put the room itself. That honor belongs to Sarah Winchester.

In 1880, she inherited the Winchester Repeating Arms Company after the sudden death of her husband, William Wirt Winchester. Overwhelmed by grief, she bought a rustic eight-room house on a farm in San Jose, California. The idea was to get away from it all and keep herself busy, which she proceeded to do with great vigor.

Construction on the house never stopped. Literally. Workmen pounded away 24 hours a day, seven days a week, year after year.

Winchester was the building's sole and completely untrained architect. She "designed," if that's the right word, 750 increasingly bizarre rooms, many of which were renovated once, twice, or even a dozen times, or simply demolished, or destroyed by earthquake or fire, until a mere 160 remained at the time of her death.

How can you forget where you put a room? Just tear down walls and rearrange floor plans *ad infinitum*. Put in a total of 1000 doors, 1200 windows, 40 staircases, 47 fireplaces, and 17 chimneys (one of which ended short of the roof), plus six kitchens, two ballrooms, two basements, three elevators, and the usual complement of secret passageways.

Also make sure that many of the staircases, doors, and hallways lead nowhere. Build a window into a floor. Seal a wine cellar so that there's no way in or out.

If you opened one particular door in her house, you would walk right smack into a brick wall. If you opened another and took a single step forward, you would plunge down two stories. If you opened a third, you would find yourself looking down at a kitchen sink eight feet below.

Construction workers and servants were forced to carry detailed maps in order to find their way around. The maps were revised continually, sometimes every day. After all, it's not easy to remember where something is when nothing stays the same.

Even Mrs. Winchester, who was responsible for all the changes, couldn't remember the layout. Each morning, she gave her chief contractor the orders of the day, which she promptly forgot.

The problem only got worse as she aged along with the house, although like many people plagued by senior moments, she learned to adapt, after a fashion. She used only a few rooms, had all the servants come to her, and invited just one guest in the course of 40 years.

On the day that Mrs. Winchester died, her workmen put down their tools for the last time and walked away, never to return.

It was just as well. Had they ever entered the house again, they might never have been found.

WILLIAM BUTLER YEATS

(1865–1939)

The Irish poet and playwright William Butler Yeats was one of the central figures in 20th century literature. He was a founder of the Abbey Theatre in Dublin and the winner of a Nobel Prize in 1923. And now he's also a member of the Senior Moments Hall of Fame.

Yeats was known to put sugar in his soup and salt in his coffee. This may help to explain how he could dine without noticing what or even whether he had eaten, one of the more notable abilities shared by many Titans of Forgetfulness.

One evening at his club, Yeats saw "a clean glass and port [but] no plate" before him, and was forced to ask whether he had just eaten something without noticing. Since no one was sure, he ordered a full meal and ate it just in case.

Anything to do with dinner seemed to intensify his absentmindedness. Yeats was once holding forth about the deficiencies in T.S. Eliot's poetry when he turned to his neighbor for an opinion, only to find him holding up his place card, which read "T. S. Eliot."

Anything that Yeats ingested could slip his memory. When he was coming down with a cold, he sucked on one cough lozenge after another to soothe his throat. The lozenges were laced with opium, in an era when opiates were commonly added to nostrums. This proved to be a problem, given Yeats' absentmindedness. He paid no attention to the number he went through, until the packet was empty. He then slept for 30 hours straight.

Water also had an influence on his distractibility. While walking during a Dublin rainstorm, he was told that his raincoat was inside out. So he swiftly turned it wet side in.

Writer Katherine Tynan recalled another wet night when she and Yeats had just attended a political meeting. Try to picture them waiting for a tram, "I in my smart clothes, my high-heeled French shoes, standing in a pool of water; the wind driving the rain as it does only in a sea bound city; Willie holding the umbrella at an acute and absentminded angle which could shelter nobody."

As Yeats explained later, his mind was otherwise occupied with a poem by Shelley.

Frank O'Connor, an Irish author best known for his short stories, said that Yeats was so absorbed in his own poetry that in the middle of a conversation he would suddenly lift his right hand and beat time with it as he recited, unbidden, a few of his lines. Then he would go back to the conversation as if nothing had happened.

As Tynan wrote years later, "Yeats would come to see me, five miles from Dublin, striding over the snow-bound roads, a gaunt young figure, mouthing poetry, swinging his arms and gesticulating as he went. Dublin policemen used to eye him in those days as if uncertain whether to run him in or not."

While riding home on a bus in the throes of composition, he would often alarm the other passengers with his muttering, so much so that they would often come up to him and ask if he was all right.

On one such ride, his young daughter, Anna, accompanied him. Yeats, lost in his own world, seemed oblivious of her presence, but she knew better than to disturb him.

When they finally reached their house, she got off the bus when he did. Yeats, no doubt surprised to find someone next to him, turned to her vaguely and said, "Oh, who is it you wish to see?"

Everyone who knew Yeats learned to live with his absentmindedness. This was just as well, for there are stories of his throwing tea leaves out his kitchen window, becoming glued to fly-paper, and swallowing his hair with his spaghetti, all the while murmuring to himself, or reciting his poetry, or carrying on a conversation, talking and talking, and talking some more, whether anyone was listening or not.

THE GIFT SHOP

The Senior Moments Hall of Fame is proud to offer plaques, posters, coffee mugs, key tags, buttons, coasters, paperweights, and tee shirts and sweatshirts in all sizes. Each features a stunning artistic rendering of the Hall itself and your favorite memory quotation, selected from the list below. Whenever a fit of forgetfulness or bout of absentmindedness strikes, let your "memory keepsake" reassure you that you are not alone. (Cash only, please.)

"Put it out of your mind. In no time it will be a forgotten memory."

—*Samuel Goldwyn*

"**B**y the time you're eighty years old you've learned everything. You only have to remember it."

—*George Burns*

"**W**hen I was younger, I could remember anything, whether it had happened or not."

—*Mark Twain*

"**I**'ve a grand memory for forgetting."

—*Robert Louis Stevenson*

"**T**here are three effects of acid [LSD]: enhanced long-term memory, decreased short-term memory, and I forget the third."

—*Timothy Leary*

"**I** have the worst memory ever, so no matter who comes up to me, they're just, like, 'I can't believe you don't remember me!' I'm like, 'Oh Dad, I'm sorry!'"

—*Ellen DeGeneres*

"**A** clear conscience is usually the sign of a bad memory."

—*Stephen Wright*

"**T**he face is familiar, but I can't remember my name."

—*Robert Benchley*

"**Y**ou're getting old when you see a girl who looks like someone you used to know, and it turns out to be her daughter."

—*Mike Connolly*

"**W**hy is it that our memory is good enough to retain the least triviality that happens to us, and yet not good enough to recollect how often we have told it to the same person?"

—*François de La Rouchefoucauld*

"**H**ere's a way [you] can easily kill a good half hour. One, place your car keys in your right hand. Two, with your left hand, call a friend and confirm a lunch or dinner date. Three, hang up the phone. Four, now look for your keys."

—*Steve Martin*

"**H**appiness is nothing more than good health and a bad memory."

—*Albert Schweitzer*

"**N**othing is more responsible for the 'good old days' than a bad memory."

—*Franklin Pierce Adams*

"As I was leaving this morning, I said to myself, 'The last thing you must do is forget your speech.' And sure enough, as I left the house this morning, the last thing I did was to forget my speech."

—*Rowan Atkinson*

"I write down everything I want to remember. That way, instead of spending a lot of time trying to remember what it is I wrote down, I spend the time looking for the paper I wrote it down on."

—*Beryl Pfizer*

"Ever stop to think, and forget to start again?"

—*Graham Weeks*

"Interestingly, according to modern astronomers, space is finite. This is a very comforting thought, especially for people who can never remember where they left things."

—*Woody Allen*

"If I could remember your name, I'd ask you where I left my keys."

—*Bumper Sticker*

"**I** don't remember anybody's name. How do you think the 'dahling' thing got started?"

—Zsa Zsa Gabor

"**I** am ninety-five. I still chase girls, but I can't remember why."

—George Burns

"**In** boxing, you have to prepare for memory loss. I wanted to make sure I didn't forget anybody's name."

—George Foreman, who named all his sons George

"**The** memories of my family outings are still a source of strength to me. I remember we'd all pile into the car—I forget what kind it was... I'm not sure where we'd go, but I think there were some trees there... I remember a bigger, older guy we called 'Dad'... I guess some things never leave you."

—Jack Handey

BIBLIOGRAPHICAL NOTE

This is a book of non-fiction, and as such, everything in it is true. Hopefully. However, since histories, diaries, correspondence, periodicals, Web sites, biographies, and autobiographies are often based on people's memory, and memory, as we well know, can be a bit hazy at times, one must ultimately judge the reliability of anecdotes by cross-checking them as much as possible and go on from there. To that end, the material in this book has been adapted from a great number of sources (too many to remember, frankly, or list, and more than enough to bore you senseless), but in case you're interested, here are some of them: "Absent-mindedness," by Lyle Larsen; *America's First Families*, by Carl Sferrazza Anthony (Touchstone, 2000); *Bartlett's Book of Anecdotes*, edited by Clifton Fadiman and André Bernard (Little, Brown & Co., 2000); *Baseball Anecdotes*, by Daniel Okrent and Steve Wulf (Oxford University Press, 1989); *The Book of Musical Anecdotes*, by Norman Lebrecht (The Free Press, 1985); *Broadway Anecdotes*, by Peter Hay (Oxford University Press, 1989); *British Literary Anecdotes*, by Robert Hendrickson (Facts on File, 1990); *The Bumper Book of Operatic Disasters*, by Hugh Vickers (Pan Books, 1998); *Congressional Anecdotes*, by Paul F. Boller, Jr. (Oxford University Press, 1992); *Cruel and Unusual Puns*, by Don Hauptman (Dell Publishing, 1991);

Eccentric Lives, Peculiar Notions, by John Michell (Black Dog & Leventhal Publishers, distributed by Workman Publishing, 1999); *Eccentrics*, by Dr. David Weeks and Jamie James (Kodansha America, 1996); *The Emperor of the United States of America and Other Magnificent English Eccentrics*, by Catherine Caufield (Routledge & Kegan Paul, 1981); *English Eccentrics*, by Edith Sitwell (Faber and Faber, 1933); "Famous Puzzles of Great Mathematicians," by Miodrag Petkovic; *Forever, Erma*, by Erma Bombeck (Andrews, McMeel, 1997); *Funny Peculiar*, by Aubrey Dillon Malone (Prion, 2001); *Goldwyn*, by A. Scott Berg (Alfred A. Knopf, 1989); *Governor Reagan*, by Lou Cannon (PublicAffairs Books, 2003); *Great Country House Disasters*, by Hugh Vickers and Caroline McCullough (Macmillan, 1982); *The Greatest Science Stories Never Told*, by Rick Beyer (Harper Collins, 2009); *The Greatest Presidential Stories Never Told*, by Rick Beyer (Harper Collins, 2007); *The Greatest War Stories Never Told*, by Rick Beyer (Harper Collins, 2005); *The Guinness Book of Humorous Anecdotes*, by Nigel Rees (Guinness Publishing, 1994); *The Hollywood Book of Extravagance*, by James Robert Parish (John Wiley & Sons, 2007); *How to Live: Or a Life of Montaigne in One Question and Twenty Attempts at an Answer*, by Sarah Blakewell (Other Press, 2010); *The Hypochondriacs*, by Brian Dillon (Faber and Faber, 2009); *If You Don't Have Anything Nice to Say, Come Sit Next to Me*, by Coral Amende (Macmillan, 1994); *Jazz Anecdotes*, by Bill Crow (Oxford University Press, 1990); *Lives of the Artists*, by Giorgio Vasari, translated by

Mrs. Jonathan Foster (Dover Publications, 2005); *The Man Who Ate Bluebottles*, by Catherine Caufield (Icon Books, 1981); *The Man Who Loved Only Numbers*, by Paul Hoffman (Hyperion, 1998); *Michel de Montaigne*, by Edith Sichel (Kennikat Press, 1911); *Michel de Montaigne: The Complete Essays*, Michel Montaigne, translated and edited by M.A. Screech (Penguin Classics, 1993); *Mathematics: People, Problems, Results*, by Douglas M. Campbell (Wadsworth Publishing, 1984); *My Favorite Intermissions*, by Victor Borge (Dorset Press, 1971); *The New Oxford Book of Literary Anecdotes*, edited by John Gross (Oxford University Press, 2006); Norbert Wiener Anecdotes, collected by Howard Eves; *Opera Anecdotes*, by Ethan Mordden (Oxford University Press, 1995); *The Outline of Sanity: A Life of G.K. Chesterton*, by Alzina Stone Dale (William B. Eerdmans Publishing, 1982); *The Oxford Book of Legal Anecdotes*, (Oxford University Press, 1986); *The Oxford Book of Military Anecdotes*, edited by Max Hastings (Oxford University Press, 1985); *The Oxford Book of Royal Anecdotes*, edited by Elizabeth Longford (Oxford University Press, 1989); *Pardon Me, But You're Eating My Doily*, by Robert Morley (St. Martin's Press, 1983); *Peculiar People*, by Augustus Hare (Academy Chicago Publishers, 1995); *Presidential Anecdotes*, by Paul F. Boller, Jr. (Oxford University Press, 1981); *Presidential Wives*, by Paul F. Boller, Jr. (Oxford University Press, 1988); *The Private Lives of the Impressionists*, by Sue Roe (Harper Collins, 2006); "Recollections of a Chinese Physicist," by C.K. Jen (Los Alamos, New Mexico, 1990); *Robert Morley's Book of Bricks*, by Robert Morley (G.P. Putnam's Sons, 1979); *The Scientists*, by John Gribbin (Random House, 2002); *Secret Lives of Great Artists*, by Elizabeth Lunday (Quirk Books, 2008); *Secret Lives of Great Authors*, by Robert Schnakenberg (Quirk Books, 2008); *Secret Lives of the Supreme Court*, by Robert Schnakenberg (Quirk Books, 2008); *Secret Lives of the U.S. Presidents*, by Cormac O'Brien (Quirk Books, 2004); *Slonimsky's Book of Musical Anecdotes*, by Nicholas Slonimsky (Schirmer Books, 1948); "Some Mathematicians I Have Known," by George Pólya, Stanford University; *Stupid History*, by Leland Gregory (Andrews, McMeel Publishing, 2007); *Taken Care Of: The Autobiography of Edith Sitwell* (Atheneum, 1965); "Teaching and History of Mathematics in the United States," by F. Cajori; *Theatrical Anecdotes*, by Peter Hay (Oxford University Press, 1987); *Try and Stop me*, by Bennett Cerf (Simon & Schuster, 1945); *Unusually Stupid Politicians*, by Kathryn Petras and Ross Petras (Villard, 2007); *The Worldly Philosophers*, by Robert L. Heilbroner (Simon & Schuster, 1953); *Written Lives*, by Javier Marías (New Directions, 1999); *You Lose Some, You Lose Some*, by Eric Furman & Lou Harry (Ennis Books, 2004); and Anecdotage.com.

PHOTO CREDITS

The cover image is a modified version of a 19th century lithograph in the public domain. The images of the following are part of the Wikimedia Commons collection, not under copyright, and in the public domain: Ampère, Beethoven, Borodin, Bowles, Bruckner, Dirac, Einstein, Goldwyn, Goodman, La Fontaine, Landor, Montaigne, Monroe, Newton, Porson, Sackville-West, Salmon, Scriabin, Smith, Spooner, Sylvester, Taft, Terry, and Wiener. The lithograph of George Harvest's church was first published in 1824 and is not under copyright. The photos of Brando, Dole, Ford, Nixon, Taft, and Waddell are part of U.S government archives and available for public use. The original photo of Gielgud was taken by Allan Warren and made publicly available under a Creative Commons license. The image of Erma Bombeck is from a window display at the Erma Bombeck Writers' Workshop. The photos of Chesterton and Herriot were never copyrighted. The photo of Matthews is a screen shot taken during a television broadcast. The original image of Winchester is part of the San Jose Research Library collection. The original photo of Yeats was taken by George Charles Beresford and is in the public domain. The gift shop logo is available for unrestricted use.

AUTHOR AND SENIOR CURATOR

Tom Friedman has written four books. Two are humor books about senior moments — the best-selling *1000 Unforgettable Senior Moments* (Workman Publishing, 2006) with over 350,000 copies in print and *The Senior Moments Memory Workout* (Sterling Publishing, 2010). The other two are about business and economics — *Life and Death on the Corporate Battlefield* (Simon & Schuster, 1982), written with Paul Solman, and *Up the Ladder* (Warner Books, 1986). But mostly he's worked in public television. For nearly 25 years, he served as an executive producer, senior producer, producer, and writer at WGBH Boston, the station responsible for one-third of PBS programming. For the science series, *Odyssey of Life*, he won the George Foster Peabody Award, the Pulitzer Prize of broadcasting. He has literally dozens of television credits and a handful of other awards, which, if he is pressed, he may or may not be able to recall, depending on the day. This is first job as a museum curator.